Kevan and Ellis
on
Credit Hire

KEVAN AND ELLIS
ON
CREDIT HIRE

Tim Kevan
Barrister, Middle Temple
MA (Hons)(Cantab)

and

Aidan Ellis
Barrister, Middle Temple
MA (Cantab)

© Tim Kevan and Aidan Ellis 2008

Published by

xpl publishing
99 Hatfield Road
St Albans AL1 4JL
UK

www.xplpublishing.com

ISBN 978 1 85811 395 1

Printed and typeset in the UK

CONTENTS

FOREWORD

I am honoured to be asked to contribute a foreword to the new edition of Credit Hire by my friends and former pupils, Tim Kevan and Aidan Ellis. I taught them both when they were undergraduates at, respectively, Magdalene and Downing Colleges, Cambridge. When I did so, I was in no doubt that each would forge for himself a successful career in practice at the Bar of England and Wales. And so they both have and continue to do.

Their legal expertise is further indicated by the fact that the book is now in its third edition. Written originally by Tim Kevan alone, it is now in the joint and sure hands of its original author and Aidan Ellis and brings credit to them both. I am bound to say that, before reading it, Credit Hire was, to me, *tabula rasa*. As the learned authors might no doubt put it to me, to parody the language of the great F.E. Smith, "we are in little doubt that you are none the wiser on the subject for having done so. We have long since ceased to hope for, still less to expect the impossible. But we trust that you are somewhat better informed". And so I am. It is clear to me that the book is both succinctly and clearly written and I am in doubt that it has been and will continue to be of great utility and help to those who are struggling to practice in this arcane area.

I should add that to see old pupils flourishing in their chosen career, as Tim Kevan and Aidan Ellis so clearly are both in practice and in print brings the greatest pleasure to a retired and aging don.

John Hopkins
Downing College
Cambridge

PREFACE

This book is aimed at anyone who has any involvement with the credit hire industry from garages and credit hire company employees to insurance claims handlers, solicitors and barristers. So, too, perhaps for those litigants curious enough to want to find out about the battle in which they have innocently become involved following a road traffic accident. It is hoped that it will be of help both to those tackling the subject for the first time and to those experienced in its most intricate details.

The death of credit hire litigation has been predicted on numerous occasions in the past ten years. In particular following the decisions in *Dimond v Lovell* and later *Clark v Ardington and others* it was thought that credit hire litigation would simply dry up.

It lives. Indeed it prospers. There are still credit hire cases coming before the County Courts every day. True the battleground has shifted over the years. Early editions of this book were largely concerned with the technical arguments based on the Consumer Credit Act 1974. These were adjudicated on finally in *Dimond v Lovell*. Since then most if not all credit hire companies have drafted their agreements to avoid regulation under the Consumer Credit Act 1974. There were teething problems with the new agreements, largely covered at chapter 3. With a few exceptions, in practice the consumer credit arguments are now largely a thing of the past.

More frequently the arguments fought in courts today revolve around the newer decisions. County courts are asked to determine whether Claimants are impecunious within the meaning of *Lagden v O'Connor* or whether rates evidence is admissible or probative pursuant to *Burdis v Livsey*. Thus for the lawyer about to step into court on his / her first credit hire case, the most important chapters are probably chapters 8 – 10. The earlier chapters have also been revised and updated to maintain their relevance to contemporary issues.

It was always intended to produce a third edition of this book following the Court of Appeal decision in *Burdis v Livsey*. In the meantime there have been other major developments such as the House of Lords' ruling on impecuniosity in *Lagden v O'Connor* and Parliament's adoption of the Consumer Credit Act 2006.

The law is stated as it is understood by the authors as at 31 January 2008. Any errors are the authors' own for which we apologise and would hope to correct by the next edition. The purpose of this book is to highlight the various areas of law potentially associated with credit hire. It is not intended to be a substitute for legal advice and readers researching a particular problem should not rely upon its contents in isolation but should instead refer to textbooks on the particular aspect of the problem and to legally qualified professionals.

Thanks are due to our colleagues in Chambers at 1 Temple Gardens. In particular to Jonathan Hough, Marcus Grant, Dominic Adamson, Paul McGrath and Tim Sharpe among others. We are also grateful to Roland Waters and Anthony Johnson for their original ideas and research into Chapter 12.

TABLE OF CASES

TABLE OF STATUTES

Chapter 1

CHAMPERTY

The law of champerty makes an interesting study in legal history. In essence it consists of wrongfully interfering in the disputes of others. Champerty originated to *"resist the oppression of private individuals through suits fomented and sustained by unscrupulous men of power"* (Lord Mustill in *Giles v Thompson* [1994] AC 142 at 153). It was both a crime and a tort. Its importance faded over time as the courts developed other mechanisms to avoid abuses. Finally, on the recommendation of the Law Commission, Parliament abolished the crimes and torts of champerty and maintenance by section 14 of the Criminal Law Act 1967. Section 14(2) provided one exception, that the abolition of criminal and civil liability, *"shall not affect any rule of [law] as to the cases in which a contract is to be treated as contrary to public policy or otherwise illegal."*

This provided the window in *Giles v Thompson,* for the Defendant insurers to argue that the credit hire contracts were champertous because the credit hire companies were instigating the litigation, had a financial interest in the outcome and often were funding them. Therefore, they argued, the agreements were illegal and unenforceable against the Claimant. Which, they went on to say, meant that the charges could not be recovered from the Defendant.

This was dismissed by the House of Lords. Lord Mustill gave the leading speech, although he drew heavily on the judgment of Steyn LJ in the Court of Appeal which had set out the historical roots of the law of champerty. He noted that the law of champerty has retained importance in two distinct areas of law. First, it remains a rule of professional conduct for a solicitor not to accept payment from a claimant calculated as a proportion of the sum recovered from the Defendant. Second, champerty is relevant to the assignment of bare rights of action. Broadly speaking in these two areas the court will consider whether the transaction bears the hallmarks of champerty. If it does, it is prima facie unlawful unless it can be validated by the third party having a legitimate interest in supporting the action.

Lord Mustill however refused to apply this two stage test to the credit hire cases. Rather he asked the single question whether there is:

> wanton and officious intermeddling with the disputes of others in where the meddler has no interest whatever, and where the assistance he render to one party or the other is without justification or excuse.

This is essentially a question of fact. Consideration must be given to all aspects of a transaction. At all times the court must bear in mind that the public policy behind the law of champerty is to *"protect the purity of justice and the interests of vulnerable litigants"*.

The House of Lords held that the credit hire agreements were not champertous. There was no realistic prospect of the administration of justice suffering. Where the Claimant retained what Steyn LJ had termed a *"residual liability"* to pay for the hire charges, the contract would be enforceable. It was not right to say that the company was taking a share of the proceeds of litigation, rather the fruits of litigation provided a source from which the motorist could satisfy his liability to the company. This was the case provided that the Claimant retained a liability to pay for the hire charges whether he won or lost the case against the other side. In *Giles v Thompson* this was held to be so in all of the cases despite the fact that in at least one of them, the publicity material had suggested the cars were free.

In the later case of *De Crittenden v Bayliss* [2002] EWCA Civ 50, the Court of Appeal were asked to determine whether an agreement was champertous. The Claimant and Defendant shared business interests. The Defendant was involved in litigation which, if he lost, would have damaged his financial standing and hence the Claimant's business interests. The Claimant agreed with the Defendant that he would assist him with the litigation in return for 50% of the proceeds. The two later fell out and the Claimant sued on the contract. The Defendant argued that it was champertous and hence unenforceable.

The Court of Appeal followed Lord Mustill's approach to champerty in *Giles*. Looking at the case as a whole, the Claimant did have a proper interest in the case aside from his share of the proceeds. The Claimant was not a solicitor and so was not caught by the more stringent rules that apply to solicitors by virtue of their importance as officers of the court. Further the litigation overall was being conducted by a solicitor, such that the Claimant could not have endangered the administration of justice. Accordingly the agreement was not champertous.

Impact on the Industry

Giles v Thompson was a watershed since it legitimised the credit hire industry and sparked its commercial growth. It seemed that all credit hire companies needed to do to succeed was to ensure that there was a residual liability on the Claimant. As a result, the argument of champerty in credit hire cases has largely died out. Champerty remains relevant to issues of solicitors' costs (about which there is a whole body of case law which is outside the scope of this book) and assignments of rights of action.

For insurers, it was time to turn to new arguments against the credit hire companies. The stakes were high because the insurers claimed to be paying millions of pounds in credit hire charges annually. Points about mitigation of loss began to be taken. Further at [1993] 3 All ER 321, 365A–B, Lord Mustill commented that he did not think that this burgeoning industry was best regulated by an invocation of the law of champerty. Instead, he thought that it could more appropriately be regulated by the consumer protection laws. The portent of the words can only be seen with the luxury of hindsight. It was not until June 1997 that the first successful defence involving the Consumer Credit Act 1974 was reported in any journal (*Smerdon v Ellis* [1997] 6 CL).

Numerous cases were reported in Current Law and eventually, the County Courts started to be clogged with credit hire cases, some lasting a day in the small claims court with lengthy skeleton arguments having been exchanged on both sides. A debate started and Judges started taking sides according to their view of the law. It was a peculiar anomaly that whilst the Consumer Credit Act arguments were mostly succeeding in the South of England, they appeared to be invariably failing in the North.

Chapter 2

CONSUMER CREDIT ACT 1974

After jostling for position in the County Courts, eventually a test case was selected to proceed through the higher courts on the consumer credit issue. That case was *Dimond* v *Lovell*. It involved a credit hire contract with First Automotive and was an appeal from a judgment of Recorder Anton Lodge QC in Sheffield County Court. The issues were divided into three parts:

a) the Consumer Credit Act 1974
b) the residual liability question
c) mitigation of loss / rates

The first part of *Dimond* v *Lovell* in both the Court of Appeal and the House of Lords concerned whether the credit hire contract in question was regulated by the Consumer Credit Act 1974. In order to understand this, it is necessary to look at the structure of the Act in some detail and sections 8 – 15 in particular. We shall first set out the analysis of Scott V-C who gave the leading judgment in the Court of Appeal and then have a look at some of the speeches in the House of Lords.

Does it involve "credit"?

Section 9 defines "credit" as follows:

> (1)In this Act "credit" includes a cash loan, and any other form of financial accommodation.

Scott V–C examined the numerous arguments for and against whether the contract involved credit. At paragraph 56, he quoted from Volume 1 of Consumer Credit Legislation, edited by Professor Goode:

> Debt is deferred, and credit extended, whenever the contract provides for the debtor to pay, or gives him the option to pay, later than the time at which payment would otherwise have been earned under the express or implied terms of the contract.

At paragraph 57, he continued:

> This principle, in my judgment, correctly expresses the test for identifying "credit" for the purposes of the 1974 Act.

At paragraph 59, he stated:

> These statements of principle, applied to the facts of the present case, seem to me to require the conclusion, a conclusion which common sense demands, that in allowing payment for the replacement vehicle to be deferred until her damages claim was concluded, Mrs Dimond was being allowed credit.

There were numerous technical arguments against such a conclusion. In particular, those provided by Professor Goode who Scott V–C (at paragraph 64) described as, "an acknowledged master of the intricacies of consumer credit control". However, he continued:

> Nonetheless I am unable to accept this analysis. First, the proposition that a car hire agreement does not involve the acquisition of a service is not in my judgment, correct. A car hire company offers a service to its customers just as does a company that hires out video tapes, a liveryman who hires out horses or Moss Bros in hiring out evening dress. There is, in my opinion, no distinction in principle between a service that consists of making available some article for use by a customer and the service offered by a barber or by a taxi driver or a caterer. If any of these services is made available on terms that involve deferring payment for a period after the service has come to an end, the supplier of the service is, in my opinion, providing a credit facility to the customer. In the present case, the agreement that Mrs Dimond's obligation to pay for the car hire would be deferred until her damages claim has been concluded was, in my judgment, an agreement allowing her "credit" for the purposes of the 1974 Act.

What type of credit is it?

Section 10 provides:

> (1)   for the purposes of this Act –
> (a) running-account credit is a facility under a personal credit agreement whereby the debtor is enabled to receive from time to time (whether in his own person, or by another person) from the creditor or a third party cash, goods and services (or any of them) to an amount or value such that, taking into account payments made by or to the credit of the debtor, the credit limit (if any) is not at any time exceeded; and

(b)fixed sum credit is any other facility under a personal credit agreement whereby the debtor is enabled to receive credit (whether in one amount or by instalments).

At paragraph 27, Scott V–C stated, "It seems clear to me that 1st Automotive's agreement does not allow its customers "running account credit" as described in section 10(1)(a). It follows that, if the agreement is a personal credit agreement, it allows fixed sum credit as described in section 10(1)(b)."

What type of credit agreement is it?

Section 8 provides:

> (1)   A consumer credit agreement is an agreement between an individual ("the debtor") and any other person ("the creditor") by which the creditor provides the debtor with credit of any amount.

Scott V-C concluded at paragraph 69 that the agreement was a personal credit agreement and a consumer credit agreement.

Section 11(1) provides:

> A restricted-use credit agreement is a regulated consumer credit agreement –
> (a) to finance a transaction between the debtor and the creditor, whether forming part of that agreement or not, or
> (b) to finance a transaction between the debtor and a person (the 'supplier') other than the creditor, or
> (c) to refinance any existing transaction of the debtor's, whether to the creditor or another person,
> and "restricted-use credit" shall be construed accordingly.

Scott V–C concluded at paragraph 29:

> The arrangement between Mrs Dimond and 1st Automotive did not involve the re-financing of any existing indebtedness. It involved the postponement of the time for payment of an indebtedness, namely, the hire charges. The charges were payable and the indebtedness was created under the same transaction as provided for the postponement of the time for payment. There was no re-financing. The agreement postponing the time for payment was, in my opinion, for section 11 purposes, an agreement for financing a transaction between Mrs Dimond and 1st Automotive. If it was a consumer credit agreement it was caught by section 11(1)(a), not section 11(1)(c).

Section 12 defines the expression "debtor-creditor-supplier-agreement". It provides:

> A debtor-creditor-supplier agreement is a regulated consumer credit
> agreement being –
>> (a)   a restricted-use credit agreement which falls within section
>> 11(1)(a), or
>> (b)   ... . ., or
>
> ...

At paragraph 31, Scott V–C stated, "So, if the 1st Automotive agreement is a consumer credit agreement, it is a debtor-creditor-supplier agreement under section 12".

For the sake of completeness, he went on in paragraph 32 to state that, "Nothing for the present purposes turns, in my opinion, on sections 13 and 14."

Is it also a consumer hire agreement?

Section 15 defines the expression "consumer hire agreement". It provides:

> (1)   A consumer hire agreement is an agreement made by a person with
> an individual (the "hirer") for the bailment ... of goods to the hirer, being an
> agreement which –
>
> (a)   is not a hire-purchase agreement and
>
> (b)   is capable of subsisting for more than three months, and
>
> (c)   does not require the hirer to make payments exceeding £15,000.
>
> (2) A consumer hire agreement is a regulated agreement if it is not an
> exempt agreement.

Without a great deal of analysis on this point, Scott V–C in the Court of Appeal concluded at paragraph 34 that:

> [1st Automotive's agreement] is beyond question an agreement for the
> bailment of goods to the hirer. But it is not capable of subsisting for more
> than three months. Condition 19 [of the agreement] limits its duration to 28
> days. So the agreement is not a consumer hire agreement under section 15.

It seems that the subtleties of the section were not argued before the Court of Appeal. For example, it might have been argued by the Defendant that the three months referred to the agreement not the bailment and that the credit agreement itself was capable of subsisting for more than three months. Further, it could have been argued by the Claimant that the agreement did not provide for the bailment of goods but instead for the provision of services and that the two are different.

Some of these points were resolved in *Burdis* v *Livsey* [2003] QB 36. It was argued by the Defendant that although the hire is restricted to a period not exceeding twelve weeks, liability to pay under the agreement subsists for more than three months. The Court of Appeal concluded at paragraph 48 that "Section 15 is directed at the long-term bailment of goods which are not the subject of hire purchase agreements. Sub-section (1)(b) is intended to refer to the period of such bailment and not to any other obligations which might be assumed under the agreement." Accordingly the agreement was not a consumer hire agreement unless the bailment was capable of subsisting for more than three months.

The Claimant in *Dimond* also raised the argument that it was not possible for an agreement to be both a regulated consumer credit agreement and at the same time a regulated consumer hire agreement since the Act had differing requirements for each. In support, the Claimant referred to the Consumer Credit (Agreements) Regulations 1983.

At paragraph 48, Scott V–C commented:

> I am very doubtful, however, whether it is proper to attempt to construe the 1974 Act in the context of the 1983 Regulations. It is certainly right to try and construe the 1974 Act as a whole. But the 1983 Regulations post-dated the Act by some 9 years and I do not think the content of the Regulations can be taken to be a guide to what Parliament intended by the language used in the Act.

At paragraph 67, he went on:

> [I] am not persuaded that the two regimes would necessarily be incompatible. If certain prescribed requirements have to be included in regulated agreements for the hire of goods and other requirements have to be included in regulated agreements that provide credit, then agreements that both provide for the hire of goods and allow credit for payment of the hire charges may have to include both sets of requirements. If any genuine case of incompatibility were to arise, the Act provides the remedy via an application under section 60(3) for a waiver or variation of the requirements [see below].

Scott V–C, without submissions having been given on the section, referred to section 18 of the Act which expressly provides that agreements may be caught by both regimes.

Conclusion: what type of agreement is a credit hire agreement?

At paragraphs 68–69, Scott V–C concluded:

> I prefer an answer to this first question that confronts the potential two regimes difficulty [for which, see below] to one that ignores the obvious credit facility being provided to customers under agreements like 1st Automotive's and that distorts the otherwise clear language of the statutory definitions in sections 8, 9, 10, 11 and 12 of the Act.

> In my judgment the 1st Automotive agreement was a personal credit agreement (section 8(1)), a consumer credit agreement (section 8(2)), an agreement for a fixed sum credit facility (section 10(1)(b)), a restricted-use credit agreement under section 11(1)(a) and a debtor-creditor-supplier agreement under section 12(a). It would also have been a consumer hire agreement if it had been capable of lasting more than 3 months.

The House of Lords

Lord Hoffman

The House of Lords unanimously upheld the Court of Appeal's decision that the credit hire contract in question provided credit and was regulated within the meaning of the Act. However the reasoning differed from that of Scott V–C in the Court of Appeal.

As Lord Hoffman stated in the leading speech (at page 394):

> My Lords, it seems to me that one emerges from these statutory thickets holding onto a very simple question. Did 1st Automotive provide Mrs Dimond with credit? If so, the hiring agreement was a personal credit agreement and since, it was for a good deal less than £15,000, a consumer credit agreement and thus (subject to the question of exemption) a regulated agreement.

He commented upon the contract in question:

> So, according to the terms of the contract, 1st Automotive "allow[s] the hirer credit on the hire charges" this arrangement is described as a "credit

facility" and if there is a breach of condition 5(iii) the "credit allowed" may be terminated. This is unpromising material for an argument.

He went on to quote the definition of credit by Professor Goode (Goode, Consumer Credit Legislation, loose leaf ed., vol 1, para. 443), relied upon by the Defendant and approved by the Court of Appeal, without criticising it:

> credit [is] extended whenever the contract provides for the debtor to pay, or gives him the option to pay, later than the time at which payment would otherwise have been earned under the express or implied terms of the contract.

The Defendant, he reported, said that in the absence of credit terms, hire would have been payable *per diem in diem* during the hiring period or, at the latest, when it ended. Allowing the hirer to defer payment until the claim for damages had been concluded was providing credit.

The Appellant argued that the services provided to Mrs. Dimond were not only the use of the car but also the pursuit of her claim. These obligations should be treated as forming part of an entire contract in which 1st Automotive could not recover any part of the consideration until it had not only allowed Mrs. Dimond the use of the car but also brought the claim for damages to a conclusion. Only at this point would 1st Automotive become entitled to payment and therefore the provision for "credit" was not really credit at all. Payment was not postponed beyond the date at which it would in any event have first become payable.

Lord Hoffman did not dismiss this argument out of hand but said that:

> This argument depends upon construing the contract as imposing upon 1st Automotive a duty to Mrs. Dimond to pursue the claim and treating the performance of that duty as forming part of an entire contract which also included the provision of the vehicle.

He went on:

> In my opinion there was no misuse of language when the contract described clause 5(i) as a credit facility. The only obligation of 1st Automotive under the agreement was to provide the vehicle. In the absence of credit, it would have been entitled to payment during or at the end of the hire. All the provisions about the pursuit of the claim were express or implied conditions that deferred the right to recover the hire and therefore constituted a granting of credit. In addition, of course, the pursuit of the claim by 1st Automotive on behalf of Mrs. Dimond may have given rise to further obligations to her, such as the obligation to indemnify her against a liability

for costs which Lord Mustill mentions in *Giles* v. *Thompson* [1994] 1 A.C. 142, 163.

By implication, Lords Browne-Wilkinson, Nicholls and Saville agreed with the analysis of Lord Hoffman on this point.

This potentially might leave it open for Claimants or credit hire companies to argue with different contracts that there was a positive duty to "pursue the claim" and that the performance of that duty should be treated as forming part of an entire contract which also included the provision of the vehicle. In the main, however, these arguments have not been pursued.

Two cases which Defendants may be able to use in any event to support an argument that credit is given where someone hires out a car without insisting on payment until the termination of the hire are: *R* v *Jones* [1898] 1 QB 119 at 124-5 and *Fisher* v *Raven* [1964] AC 210 at 232. So, too, they may rely upon *R* v *Peters* [1885] 16 QB 636 as discussed in *R* v *Miller* [1977] 1 WLR 1129 at 1133E-1134F as an example of a similar situation where at common law credit was deemed to have been obtained. Also useful may be the analysis of Lord Mustill in *Giles* v *Thompson* (*Devlin* v *Baslington*) [1994] 1 AC 142 at 160G-H.

Lord Hobhouse
Lord Hobhouse took a slightly different approach to this issue. He stated (at page 405):

> I agree with your Lordships that this agreement did involve the provision of credit. The answer to that question is not provided by the application of some formula but rather by looking at the terms of the agreement in the context of the relevant transaction as a whole. Here the terms of the agreement are explicit. The lessor is extending credit to the hirer. It is described as a "credit facility" and the allowance of credit and its termination are specifically referred to. Under these circumstances there can be no escape from the answer which your Lordships have given.

However, he made a qualification to the comments of Lord Hoffman:

> I would add only one further comment. The test formulated by Professor Goode adopted by the Vice Chancellor in the Court of Appeal [1999] 3 W.L.R. 561, 572 will not always be a satisfactory one to apply. Many commercial agreements contain provisions which could be said to postpone (or advance) the time at which payment has to be made. Frequently, there will be reasons for this other than the provision of credit. Payment may be postponed as security for the performance of some other obligation by the creditor. Payments may be made in advance of performance in order to tie the paying party into the commercial venture. Payment provisions may like

any other aspect of the transaction be part of its commercial structure for the division of risk, for the provision of security or simply the distribution of the commercial interest in the outcome of the transaction.

Where the transaction is a relatively simple consumer transaction little sophistication is required. The car has been hired, used and returned. No payment of the hire charges is stipulated for at that time. Payment is postponed until the hirer has been put in funds: "the lessor will allow the hirer credit on the hire charges". But neither the lessor nor the hirer is under an obligation to procure that the hirer is put in funds. The lessor has no obligation; the hirer's obligation is simply to co-operate. As is illustrated by the present case, the accident hire company itself in the contractual document characterised what it was doing as the providing a credit facility. It was clearly right to do so."

This appears to be a narrower approach to the definition of credit than Lord Hoffman. Claimants may point to this speech to support the contention that an agreement which on the face of it is a spot hire agreement, does not provide credit even though payment may not have been required or demanded. Defendants may point to the other parts of Lord Hobhouse's speech along with that of Lord Hoffman.

Section 18: multiple agreements
In the House of Lords the Claimant argued in the alternative that the agreement was a multiple agreement within the meaning of section 18 of the Act. Section 18 provides:

(1) This section applies to an agreement (a 'multiple agreement') if its terms are such as-

(a) to place a part of it within one category of agreement mentioned in this Act, and another part of it within a different category of agreement so mentioned, or within a category of agreement not so mentioned, or
(b) to place it, or a part of it, within two or more categories of agreement so mentioned.

(2) Where a part of an agreement falls within subsection (1), that part shall be treated for the purposes of this Act as a separate agreement.

(3) Where an agreement falls within subsection (1)(b), it shall be treated as an agreement in each of the categories in question, and his Act shall apply to it accordingly.

(4) Where under subsection (2) a part of a multiple agreement is to be treated as a separate agreement, the multiple agreement shall (with any necessary modifications) be construed accordingly; and any sum payable under the multiple agreement, if not apportioned by the parties, shall for the

purposes of proceedings in any court relating to the multiple agreement be apportioned by the court as may be requisite.

The argument was effectively that if credit was found to have been provided then the contract should be construed as a multiple agreement since part of it was for the provision of hire and part of it was for the provision of credit. Only the credit element, the argument went, should be unenforceable. This would still leave the hire element being unenforceable.

In response to this argument, Lord Hoffman stated (at page 396):

> I fear that I may not be able to do justice to the argument based upon this section, because I am not sure that I fully understood it ... The difficulty I have with this argument is that it seems to sever the provisions that create the debt (hiring the car) from the provisions that allow credit for payment of the debt. Whatever a multiple agreement may be, one cannot divide up a contract in that way. The creation of the debt and the terms on which it is payable must form parts of the same agreement. The truth of the matter is that I accept that the hiring agreement was a single contract. But I do not accept Mr. Wingate-Saul's submission as to what that contract was. He argues that it involved multiple obligations on the part of 1st Automotive that had to be performed over a period starting when the car was hired and ending when the damages were recovered. I consider, on the contrary, that the only primary obligation of 1st Automotive was to provide the car. The rest of the agreement dealt with the conditions upon which it would be entitled to recover the hire. To such an agreement section 18 has, of course, no relevance.

This was potentially one of the most interesting aspects of the appeal and it is unfortunate that the issue was dealt with in such a cursory fashion. Indeed, Lord Hobhouse did not explicitly deal with it at all, although in dismissing the appeal it must be assumed that he formed the view that the argument should fail.

The reasoning appears to be based upon the finding that the only obligation on the hire company was to provide a car. This is the same point which Lord Hoffman emphasised when deciding against the Claimant's arguments on whether or not credit had been provided. Therefore, once again, the finding left room for attempts to distinguish it in the future. If credit hire contracts come to court which do include such an obligation on the hire company it remains to be seen whether the court would then take a different view.

If attempts to distinguish are made, Defendants will be able to use not only the speeches in *Dimond* itself but they can also argue the underlying policy aspects of the Act.

The case of *Story and Pallister* v *National Westminster Bank* [1999] Lloyd's Rep. Bank. 261; [1999] C.C.L.R. 70, may still have significance in determining whether there is a multiple agreement in particular cases.

Multiple agreements were also raised in the Court of Appeal in *Burdis*. The Claimant argued that the obligation to pay the hire company was free standing from the clauses concerning credit. Therefore, they argued, even if the credit provisions are unenforceable the Claimant will still be obliged to pay the hire company. The Court of Appeal concluded at paragraph 60 "we do not think it is possible to regard these terms as having a free standing life of their own. They are simply part of the terms on which credit is granted."

Enforceability of the Credit Hire Agreement

Improperly executed
Section 60(1) of the Act requires the Secretary of State to "make regulations as to the form and content of documents embodying regulated agreements..."

Sub-section (2) says that:

> Regulations under subsection (1) may in particular:–

> (a) require specified information to be included in the prescribed manner in documents, and other specified material to be excluded;

> (b)contain requirements to ensure that specified information is clearly brought to the attention of the debtor or hirer, and that one part of a document is not given insufficient or excessive prominence compared with another.

Section 61 introduces the concept of a regulated agreement being "properly executed". It provides, under sub-section (1), that an agreement is not "properly executed" unless:

> (a) a document in the prescribed form itself containing all the prescribed terms and conforming to regulations under section 60(1) is signed in the prescribed manner both by the debtor or hirer and by or on behalf of the creditor or owner, and

> (b) the document embodies all the terms of the agreement, other than implied terms, and
> ...

Section 65 provides that:

> (1) An improperly-executed regulated agreement is enforceable against the debtor or hirer on an order of the court only.

Section 127(3) requires the court to dismiss an application for an enforcement order under section 65(1)

> unless a document (whether or not in the prescribed form and complying with regulations under section 60(1)) itself containing all the prescribed terms of the agreement was signed by the debtor or hirer (whether or not in the prescribed manner).

The 1974 Act was not brought into effect for a number of years. When this eventually happened it was accompanied by the Consumer Credit (Agreements) Regulations 1983 ("the 1983 Regulations") made under various sections of the Act, including sections 60, 61 and 127.

Paragraph 2 of the 1983 Regulations deals with the form and content of regulated consumer credit agreements and, by sub-paragraph (1), requires them to contain the information set out in column 2 of Schedule 1 of the 1983 Regulations. Sub-paragraph (2) catered for the situation where information about financial particulars could not be exactly ascertained and permitted "estimated information based on such assumptions as the creditor may reasonably make in all the circumstances of the case ..." to be included.

Paragraph 6(1) of the 1983 Regulations requires that:

> The terms specified in column 2 of Schedule 6 ... in relation to the type of regulated agreement referred to in column 1 ... are hereby prescribed for the purposes of section 61(1)(a) ... and of section 127(3) ...

Schedule 6 has the following entry under column 1: "Restricted-use debtor-creditor-supplier agreements for fixed sum credit ..." Against this entry under column 2 is the following prescribed term:

> A term stating the amount of credit, which may be expressed as the total cash price of the goods, services, land or other things, the acquisition of which is to be financed by credit under the agreement.

In *Dimond* v *Lovell*, it was common ground that the agreement was not, for the purposes of section 61, "properly executed" as the document signed by Mrs Dimond did not contain all the "prescribed terms" (section 61(1)(a)).

Estimating the amount of credit

It should be noted that the Claimant argued in the Court of Appeal that it would not have been possible to have included the prescribed term, i.e., the amount of credit, since the length of the hire period would be unknown. Scott V–C disagreed (at paragraph 71):

> But the daily rate of hire would be known and an estimate of the period of hire could be obtained from the garage that was repairing the damaged vehicle. In these circumstances paragraph 2(2) of the 1983 Regulations would, as I have read it, apply and would have allowed 1st Automotive to insert an estimate of the amount of credit with an indication of the assumptions on which the estimate was made. I do not accept that 1st Automotive could not have complied with the Regulations.

Waiver or variation by Director General of Fair Trading

Section 60(3) of the Act provides:

> If, on an application made to the Director [General of Fair Trading] by a person carrying on a consumer credit business or a consumer hire business, it appears to the Director impracticable for the applicant to comply with any requirement of regulations under sub-section (1) in a particular case, he may, by notice to the applicant, direct that the requirement be waived or varied in relation to such agreements ... and the regulations shall have effect accordingly.

The Claimant in *Dimond* v *Lovell* argued that the prescribed requirements that were omitted from the document signed by her could be waived or varied by the Director on an application under section 60(3). Scott V–C again disagreed (at paragraph 72):

> The proposition that a section 60(3) application can be made in order to validate an agreement already entered into where the credit has already been provided seems to me to be doubtful. Another way of putting the same point is to doubt whether a section 60(3) waiver or variation of requirements could retrospectively validate an agreement unenforceable for want of compliance with the statutory requirements. Section 60(4) seems to me to stand in the way. A subsection (3) notice would, in the case of an existing agreement, be bound to prejudice the interests of the debtor or hirer. We did not receive any detailed submissions from counsel as to whether or not an application could now be made under section 60(3) by 1st Automotive. My view, however, on a reading of sub-sections (3) and (4) is that the section 60(3) application must be made and the notice of the waiver or variation must be given to the Director before the agreement has been entered into and that the notice can have prospective but not retrospective effect.

Enforceability: conclusion

In the Court of Appeal, at paragraph 73, Scott V–C concluded:

> Accordingly, in my judgment, the agreement between Mrs Dimond and 1st
> Automotive cannot be enforced against her.

It was conceded before the House of Lords that if they found that the
agreement was regulated and presumably, if the section 18 argument failed,
then the agreement was unenforceable pursuant to sections 65 and 127 of
the 1974 Act. As set out in Chapter 5, the position would be rather different
under the Consumer Credit Act 2006. The position would now be that the
agreement would be potentially but not automatically unenforceable.

None of their Lordships went into the detail set out by Scott V-C. In
particular, they did not explicitly analyse exactly what sort of agreement it
was. However, the fact that Lord Hoffman referred to article 3(1)(a) of the
Consumer Credit (Exempt Agreements) Order 1989 implies that he decided
that the agreement was a fixed-sum debtor-creditor-supplier agreement to
which that part of the exemption order applies.

Chapter 3

EXEMPTIONS FROM THE CONSUMER CREDIT ACT

12 Month/4 Payment Exemption Clauses

In the Court of Appeal in *Dimond*, Scott V–C explicitly referred to the possibility of credit hire companies exempting their agreements from the rigours of the Act in the future. This derives from section 16 of the Act (which empowers the Secretary of State to make Regulations exempting certain types of agreement from the Act) and European legislation. The present Exemption Order is the Consumer Credit (Exempt Agreements) Order 1989 ("the Exemption Order").

Paragraph 3(1) of the Order provides:

> The Act shall not regulate a consumer credit agreement which is an agreement of one of the following descriptions, that is to say – (a) a debtor-creditor-supplier agreement being either – (i) an agreement for fixed-sum credit under which the total number of payments to be made by the debtor does not exceed four, and those payments are required to be made within a period not exceeding 12 months beginning with the date of the agreement.

Having referred to this paragraph, Scott V–C stated at paragraphs 51–52 of *Dimond* v *Lovell* that:

> Paragraph 3(1)(a)(i) shows that if, contrary to [the Claimant's] submissions, agreements like 1st Automotive's are consumer credit agreements, the hire companies can prevent them from being regulated agreements by limiting the period of credit to a maximum of 12 months.

> But that is of no relevance to 1st Automotive's agreement with Mrs Dimond which contained no limit on the duration of the "credit" save that it would terminate on the conclusion of the claim for damages.

Lord Hoffman (at page 8) provided in similar terms:

> It is however worth noticing that article 3(1)(a) of the Consumer Credit (Exempt Agreements) Order 1989 (S.I. 1989 No. 869) exempts consumer credit agreements such as this one if the total number of payments to be made by the debtor does not exceed four and "those payments are required to be made within a period not exceeding 12 months beginning with the date of the agreement.

Following the Court of Appeal judgment in *Dimond* v *Lovell*, Scott V–C's reference to the 1989 Exemption Order pointed the way to what would be the most fertile source of dispute in the months following and which eventually led to the Court of Appeal cases of *Zoan* v *Rouamba* and *Ketley* v *Gilbert*.

Numerous credit hire companies had already prepared for the contingency of a finding against 1st Automotive and had inserted clauses in their agreements which they hoped would exempt them from the rigours of the Act. In practice these disputes have now almost disappeared.

This Chapter simply sets out a summary of some of the most common arguments surrounding paragraph 3(a)(i) of the Order.

The exemption may be split into five parts. The agreement must be:

    i.   for fixed-sum credit,
    ii. under which the total number of payments to be made by the debtor does not exceed four and
    iii. those payments are required to be made
    iv. within
    v.   a period not exceeding 12 months beginning with the date of the agreement.

Exemption clauses potentially may be attacked on each of these requirements as well as on common law grounds and pursuant to the Unfair Terms in Consumer Contracts Regulations 1994 ("the 1994 Regulations") and the Unfair Terms in Consumer Contracts Regulations 1999 ("the 1999 Regulations").

Contra preferentum

Defendants may preface their submissions in this respect by stating that if there is any doubt or ambiguity as to construction, the construction most preferable to the consumer, i.e. the Claimant, rather than the credit hire company should apply. In other words the *contra preferentum* rule should be applied. See *Houghton* v *Trafalgar Insurance* [1954] 1 QB 247.

In this regard, Defendants may also point to Regulation 6 of the 1994 Regulations and Regulation 7 of the 1999 Regulations. This was accepted for example in the obiter comments of Brooke LJ in *Ketley* v *Gilbert* when he stated:

> It is not necessary to have recourse to regulation 6 of the [Unfair Terms in Consumer Contracts Regulations 1994] or to the rule, in cases of doubt, that a written instrument should be interpreted "*contra preferentum*", but if there had been any doubt in the interpretation of the agreement that doubt would have been resolved in favour of [the claimant] as the hirer, so as to render the agreement unenforceable.

This was also accepted, for example, in *Majeed* v *Incentive Group*, HHJ Ryder, Central London County Court, 27/8/1999 and *Norman* v *Selvey*, DJ Singleton [1999] 7 CL 205.

Claimants may argue that this is not like an exemption clause limiting liability and therefore the *contra preferentum* rule should not apply. Instead, it is a clause which merely takes the contract outside the complications of the Act. Further, they may argue that the *contra preferentum* rule was not designed to help insurers make windfall gains against innocent Claimants.

Claimants may also argue that contracts should be interpreted as far as possible to give effect to their commercial purpose. That purpose was to provide the Claimant with a car and for the Claimant to claim back the cost of that car from the tortfeasor. In order to fulfil this commercial purpose the contract would have to be enforceable. Reference may also be made to the rule of construction that it is better for a thing to have effect than to be made void. For example, in *Mills* v *Dunham* [1891] 1 Ch 576 at 590, it was stated:

> It is a settled canon of construction that where a clause is ambiguous a construction which will make it valid is to be preferred to one which will make it void.

In addition, Claimants may try and argue that the 1994 or 1999 Regulations do not apply for the reasons mentioned later in this chapter.

However, in the light of the comments of Brooke LJ in *Ketley* v *Gilbert*, such arguments look likely to be harder to make.

Fixed-sum credit

Some have attempted to argue that the agreement does not provide fixed-sum credit where there has been no price entered on the agreement or indeed if there was no estimate for the length of repairs as suggested by Scott V–C in the Court of Appeal. However, Scott V–C found that the agreement was for fixed-sum credit despite these inadequacies (c.f. statutory definitions cited at page 7 above). What the argument does is to highlight the difficulties with the definitions set out in the Act.

4 Payments

The argument here is that unless the agreement expressly limits the number of payments to four or less it is not exempt. The Crowther Commission which preceded the Act specifically pointed to the need to protect instalment borrowers. The original exemption order (empowered by section 16 of the Act) had no mention of twelve months. It therefore used to be simply an instalments exemption. Its importance has perhaps been forgotten with the introduction of the twelve months section. What is to stop a Claimant, Defendants may say, paying in more than four instalments in the absence of express limitation? To try and imply such limitation would be like trying to imply a twelve month clause.

Claimants may argue that in the Exemption Order, "an agreement . . . under which the total number of payments to be made by the debtor does not exceed four" the words "to be made" should be emphasised. This suggests "required to be made". However, this is not the wording and the fact that the word "required" is mentioned just one clause later in the Exemption Order, may not help this argument.

Claimants may also argue that the Act was designed to protect consumers who were otherwise contractually obliged to pay by instalments. Further, permitting payment by instalments would be an indulgence by the creditor and should not be implied where it is not expressly permitted. They may also argue that the clear intention of the agreement is to allow for one payment only.

The Defendant's argument was successful in front of at least three Circuit Judges (HHJ Ryder, *Majeed* v *Incentive Group* (above), HHJ Smithson, *Radosavljevic* v *Rufus*, Central London County Court, 23/6/1999, HHJ Russel Vick QC, *Wilson* v *Pedroz*, Medway County Court, 26/2/2001).

In *Seddon* v *Tekin* and *Dowsett* v *Clifford*, HHJ Harris, Oxford County Court, 25 August 2001, HHJ Harris stated:

> It seems to me clear that the agreement in the instant cases does not envisage instalment payments. It envisages a single payment of the hire charges "in full"…

He went on to state:

> A hirer would no doubt be free to proffer early payments as and when and as often as he chose, if for some unlikely reason he might want to, and, indeed, Helphire might accept such voluntary payments, but that does not alter the nature of the agreement itself, which is one which provides for one payment. It is thus in my judgment within the exemption of 3(1) (a) (i) of the Order. Likewise, if payment should be accepted as an indulgence outside the period stipulated in the agreement that does not alter the nature of the agreement, nor its qualification for the exception either. It merely shows that in a particular case Helphire did not insist on enforcing terms and a party to a contract may always do that. Subsequent conduct does not change the categorisation of a contract from what it was when it was made.

In *Clark* v *Ardington Electrical Services and others*, HHJ Harris, Oxford County Court, 14 September 2001, HHJ Harris followed his previous decision in *Seddon* v *Tekin* and *Dowsett* v *Clifford* and stated that:

> I adhere to what I held on that occasion notwithstanding Mr Flaux's reference to Council directive (87/102/EC). The agreement envisages payment in one go. The combination of clauses is in my view reasonably clear and it is not providing for a total number of payments to exceed four.

He went through some of the clauses and concluded:

> Those are simply not provisions for multiple payments.

At paragraph 52 of their judgment, the Court of Appeal upheld HHJ Harris on this point, saying that:

> This issue is simply one of construction of the agreements concerned. Looking at the credit hire agreement the principal obligation is contained in condition 3, the first sentence of which says when the credit period is to expire and continues "at that point you will be liable to pay". This is a one payment requirement.

Required

If the agreement leaves a discretion as to whether payment will be enforced within twelve months, Defendants may argue that this does not require payment as set down in the Order. Such arguments may be strengthened where payment has not in fact been enforced within that time. This may be used as evidence indicating the parties' contractual intention at the time of making the agreement. The point has been successful in a number of cases. *Ward* v *Murphy*, HHJ Ward, Worthing County Court, 14/9/1998 is illustrative.

Claimants may argue that any decision not to so enforce was a gratuitous indulgence on the part of the credit hire company. Alternatively, that it amounted to forbearance on the company's part. This would not amount to an extension of credit beyond the twelve months. Such an extension would require consideration. See *Joyce* v *Barlow* [1999] 2 CL and *Feary* v *Buckingham* [1999] 7 CL.

In *Seddon* v *Tekin* and *Dowsett* v *Clifford*, HHJ Harris, Oxford County Court, 25 August 2001, HHJ Harris analysed a clause which provided that, "The credit period extended by this agreement shall expire in any event 51 weeks from the date of the agreement. At the expiry of the credit period you shall then become liable to pay the hire charges in full." Another clause was in the same terms save for the time frame being 26 weeks.

He held that this came within the Exemption Order and stated:

> In my judgment the hypothetical reasonable person reading the stipulation, "You shall then become liable to pay in full" would understand that to mean that he was required to pay then and not that he may be asked to pay thereafter.

> This approach also accords with the nature of credit. In the Court of Appeal in *Dimond* v *Lovell* [1999] 3 WLR 561, the Vice Chancellor referred to *Grant* v *Watton* [1999] STC 330 and cited Pumphrey J where he said: "Credit is granted when payment is not demanded until the time later than the supply of services or goods to which the payment relates. Credit is the deferring of a payment of a sum which in the absence of an agreement would be immediately payable", and said that he entirely agreed with this. Thus at the end of the 51 or 26 weeks credit expires and the charges are immediately due and due without further demand or particularisation. The hirer, if he does not know what they are can always ask.

> The Vice Chancellor also said when considering Article 3 of the 1989 Order, "Hire companies can prevent [Consumer Credit Agreements] from being regulated agreements by limiting the period of credit to a maximum of 12 months" [1999] 3 WLR 571. Mr Williams points out that the Vice Chancellor added nothing about having explicitly to ask for payment within that period, though it is to be observed, of course, that Sir Richard Scott was

not actually dealing with this particular agreement when he said what he did.

The conclusion that I reach is also consistent with the general rule of law that payment under a contract is due without demand (see for example *Treitel on The Law of Contract* 10th edition, [1999] 677, though the matter of course is one ultimately of what the contract provides. I am somewhat fortified in my conclusion on this issue by the fact that at least six other circuit judges have made the same decision upon the same provisions. Accordingly, I find that the agreements that I have been considering were valid exempt agreements and so enforceable, and thus that the hire charges are recoverable from the defendants.

In *Clark* v *Ardington Electrical Services and others*, HHJ Harris, Oxford County Court, 14 September 2001, HHJ Harris again followed his previous decision in *Seddon* v *Tekin* and *Dowsett* v *Clifford*.

In *Pitt-Miller* v *Patel*, HHJ Marr-Johnson, Mayor's & City County Court, 24 July 2001, a clause providing that payment became "immediately due and payable... a day 51 weeks after the date of this agreement" was held to come within the Exemption Order.

Within

Potentially Defendants may also argue that payment was not required "within" the prescribed twelve months.

This issue came before the Court of Appeal in the case of *Ketley* v *Gilbert* [2001] 1 WLR 986; [2001] RTR 327; [2001] Times 17 January; [2001] ILR 19 January. The question for the court was whether the words used to describe when the hire charges fell to be repaid, namely "on the expiry of 12 months starting with the date of this agreement", satisfied the wording of the 1989 Order. The Court of Appeal held that an agreement permitting the final payment to be made "on expiry" of that period permitted the final payment to be made after the 12-month period had expired. Payment was not required to be made within a period "not exceeding 12 months" which was necessary if exemption was to be afforded to the agreement pursuant to the 1989 Order.

Where payment falls due on the anniversary of the agreement, Defendants may argue that it is not therefore due "within" the twelve months stipulated in the Order (*c.f.*, further, *Zoan* v *Rouamba* unreported 21/1/2000).

In other cases, whilst an agreement may make it clear that a credit period comes to an end before the expiration of twelve months, it may also be argued that a reasonable time to actually pay the debt would be implied for the Claimant after that date. This may then take it outside the time mentioned in the Order. This is related to the "required" point above and was accepted by HHJ Ryder in *Majeed* v *Incentive Group* (above). In this regard, it should be noted that "required" is in the passive and not the subjunctive tense in the Order suggesting a narrow approach to this word.

It is also supported by the case of *Ketley* v *Gilbert* (above). For example, at paragraph 26 of the judgment, Brooke LJ states:

> If the words of the agreement could be flexibly interpreted to permit payment a reasonable time after the expiry of 12 months (since it could not reasonably by expected that the hirer would make payment on the stroke of midnight), such payment was not required to be made within a period not exceeding 12 months, as was necessary if exemption was to be afforded to this agreement pursuant to the 1989 order.

Claimants may argue that if the credit period comes to an end, the clear implication is that payment is then due and that this would exempt an agreement. They may also refer to *ICS* v *West Bromwich BS* [1998] 1 All ER 98 and the five principles set out by Lord Hoffman (at pages 114g–115e). In particular, he stressed that the meaning which a document would convey to a reasonable man is not the same thing as the meaning of its words and where there is ambiguity, the meaning for the reasonable man should be preferred.

It was argued in the Court of Appeal in *Clark* v *Ardington*, that although the contract provided that the Claimant became liable to pay within twelve months, this is not the same as requiring payment within twelve months. The reason is that once a person becomes liable to pay, he has a reasonable time before he is actually required to pay the money. This could take it outside the twelve month period. The Court of Appeal upheld HHJ Harris is rejecting this argument. They held at paragraph 55 that "liable" may mean "bound or obliged by law" in which sense condition 14 [the relevant provision] would obviously require payment at the end of the credit period or "obliged if asked."

Twelve Months

This is the most technical of all the arguments surrounding the exemption clauses. If an agreement requires payment within twelve months "after" or "from" or "of" the date of the agreement, Defendants may argue that this does not come within the exact wording of the Order since it allows credit for one day more than that prescribed.

General rule

The general rule in counting days is for time to start the day after a specified event. In this case, it would be the day after the date of the agreement. In *Dodds* v *Walker* [1981] 1 WLR 1027, in construing section 29(3) of the Landlord and Tenant Act 1954, Lord Diplock stated:

> It is also clear under a rule that has been consistently applied by the Courts since *Lester* v *Garland* (1808) 15 VES.Jun248, that in calculating the period that has elapsed after the occurrence of the specified event such as the giving of notice, the day on which the event occurs is excluded from the reckoning. It is equally well established ... that when the relevant period is a month or a specified number of months after the giving of notice, the general rule is that the period ends on upon the corresponding date in the appropriate subsequent month ie. the day of that month that bears the same number as the day of the earlier month on which the notice was given.

See also, for example, *Goldsmiths' Co.* v *West Metropolitan Railway Co.* [1904] 1 KB 1, *Stewart* v *Chapman* [1951] 2 KB 792, *In re Lympne Investments* [1972] 1 WLR 523 and *Tanglecroft Ltd* v *Hemdale Group Ltd* [1975] 1 WLR 1545, *Carapanayoti* v *Comptori Commercial Andre* [1971] 1 Lloyds Rep. See also section 343, pages 868–873 of *Statutory Interpretation* by F.A.R. Bennion (Butterworths; 1997).

It is clear from the authorities that the general rule applies to contracts as well as statutes. See Lewison *Interpretation of Contracts*, Second Edition page 13.08, *Cartwright* v *McCormack* [1963] 1 WLR 18, *South Staffordshire Tramways Company* v *Sickness and Accident Assurance Association* [1891] 1 QB 402, paragraph 3/2/3 (at pages 14–15) of Volume 1 of the 1999 *White Book* and page 129 and 333–334 of the 1998 *Green Book*.

Therefore, if the agreement is made at midday on 1 January 2006, and payment is required to be made within twelve months "after", "from" or "of" the date of the agreement, time would start being counted at the start of 2 January 2006 and payment would be required at the end of 1 January 2007.

Exception to the general rule

In *Hare* v *Gocher* [1962] 2 QB 641 the Divisional Court had to interpret section 50(4) of the Caravan Sites and Control Development Act 1960 which provided that, "This Act shall come into force at the expiration of a period of one month beginning with the date on which it was passed". Winn J referred to Goldsmiths' and the general rule. However, in analysing the words of that particular Statute, he continued:

> It is submitted . . . I think correctly, that these words are to be taken to have
> been adopted in order to avoid equivocation, and to exclude the application
> for the purposes of the statute of the rule...which was said to be the general
> rule . . . Applying then, the exact wording . . . I am of the opinion that the
> meaning to be given . . . is that the Act shall commence, that is, come into
> force at the expiration of a period of one month, included in the
> computation of which is July 29 1960, the date on which the Statute
> received the Royal Assent. Any month of the calendar begins with the first
> of that month and does not include the first of the next month.

This is supported by the Court of Appeal case of *Trow* v *Ind Coupe* (West
Midlands) Limited [1967] 2 QB 899 in which despite Lord Denning's
dissenting judgment on the basis that this was too fine and legalistic a
distinction, the majority followed Hare. It is also supported by *Carapanayoti*
v *Comptori Commercial Andre* (above) and a number of employment cases
based upon section 67(2) of the Employment Protection (Consolidation) Act
1978 including *Cambridge University* v *Murray* [1996] ICR 460, *Haigh* v *A
Lewis & Company* (Westminster) [1973] ITR 360, *Dedman* v *British
Building & Engineering Appliances Ltd* [1974] 1 WLR 171, *B.M.K.* v *Logue*
[1993] ICR 601, *Pruden* v *Cunard Ellerman* [1993] IRLR 317, *Thompson* v
GEC Avionics [1991] IRLR 488, *Crank* v *Her Majesty's Stationery Office*
[1985] ICR 1, *T.B.A. Industrial Products* v *Morland* [1982] ICR 685; [1982]
IRLR 331. See also section 73, pages 204–206 of *Statutory Interpretation* by
F.A.R. Bennion (Butterworths; 1997).

The Exemption Order is worded in the same way and Defendants may
therefore argue that the general rule does not apply to counting the period of
time specified therein. Therefore, if the hire agreement was signed at midday
on 1 January 1999, time would start running for the Order on that day and
payment would need to be required by the end of 31 December 1999 for the
agreement to be exempt. If the general rule applied to the contract then it
would not therefore be exempt.

Again, the *contra preferentum* rule may be referred to. In particular, Lord
Esher stated in *In re North, Ex parte Hasluck* [1895] 2 QB 264 at page 270:

> ... where the computation of time is to be for the benefit of the person
> affected as much time should be given as the language admits of, and where
> it is to his detriment the language should be construed as strictly as possible.

The most significant development here is the case of *Zoan* v *Rouamba*
(above) in which the Court of Appeal held that a clause providing for
payment twelve months "after" the date of the agreement did not come
within paragraph 3 of the Consumer Credit (Exempt Agreements) Order
1989.

In particular, they found that the words in the exemption order "beginning with" meant that counting started on the day of making the agreement whereas in the absence of such a clause, counting started the day after the making of the agreement.

Claimants' arguments

After *Zoan* v *Rouamba*, the scope of any arguments with respect to the words "after", "anniversary" and probably "from" looks likely to be limited for Claimants. However, more specific arguments may arise with regard to the word "of".

In this context, it should be noted that in *Dimond* v *Lovell*, Lord Hoffman said,

> It is however worth noticing that article 3(1)(a) of the Consumer Credit (Exempt Agreements) Order 1989 (S.I. 1989 No. 869) exempts consumer credit agreements such as this one if the total number of payments to be made by the debtor does not exceed four and -"those payments are required to be made within a period not exceeding 12 months beginning with the date of the agreement." 1st Automotive can therefore obtain exemption from the Consumer Credit Act 1974 if they include a clause that requires that the hire should in any event be paid (if at all) within 12 months.

Claimants may potentially suggest that since the last sentence quoted did not mention four payments or "beginning with the date of the agreement" they are not significant. However, this issue was not before the House. Further, the statement was in the context of the previous statement where he specifically quoted the Order. In addition, Lord Hoffman did not appear to be aware of the recent Court of Appeal case of *Zoan* v *Rouamba*.

Despite these points, it remains to be seen if higher courts would rely on this statement to suggest a different interpretation of the exemption order from that in *Zoan*.

A novel argument which may be available is that at the time that the agreement was made it was contemplated that a claim for damages would be concluded within twelve months. Therefore, there was an implied term in the agreement that payment was required within the requisite twelve months.

With regard to a clause where payment was to be made "within 12 months of the date of this agreement", in *Brent* v *E.R.I. Refrigeration Limited*, HHJ Cowell, West London County Court, 8 June 2000, the court held that it came within the Exemption Order relying in particular on the cases of

Ladyman v *Wirral Estates* [1968] 2 All ER 197 and *Re Jubilee Cotton Mills* [1924] AC 958.

Defendants' Arguments

Unfair Terms in Consumer Contracts Regulations 1999

The Unfair Terms in Consumer Contracts Regulations 1999 came into force on 1 October 1999. They replaced the Unfair Terms in Consumer Contracts Regulations 1994.

The intention of the Regulations is to prevent "unfair" terms in contracts with a consumer from binding the consumer. Defendants may argue that a clause purporting to exempt an agreement from the Consumer Credit Act is such a term. It is designed to oust consumer protection legislation and therefore limits the rights of the consumer. Such an argument was accepted by DJ White in *Kersley* v *Vincent*, Taunton County Court, 28/8/1999. The Defendant's point may be strengthened where there is no warning to the Claimant as to what he is signing up to and in particular as to the significance of the clause exempting the agreement from the Act.

When considering the potential role of the 1999 Regulations, there are essentially two questions: do the fairness provisions of the 1999 Regulations apply to the term in question and is the term unfair?

Application of the Fairness Provisions in the 1999 Regulations

The 1999 Regulations apply to "unfair terms in contracts concluded between a seller or a supplier and a consumer" (Regulation 4(1)). Regulation 3(1) defines both "supplier" and "consumer". There is no doubt that a credit hire company is a supplier within the meaning of the Regulations. The definition of consumer is: "any natural person who, in contracts covered by these Regulations, is acting for purposes which are outside his trade, business or profession." Thus the Regulations only protect natural persons: a company which hires a vehicle, even if it acts for purposes outside its business, cannot rely on the Regulations.

The Regulations only apply to terms which have not been individually negotiated (*c.f.* Regulation 5(1)). The burden of proof is on the supplier to show that a term was individually negotiated (Regulation 5(4)).

Certain terms in contracts are exempt from scrutiny on the 1999 Regulations. Regulation 4(2) provides that:

> these Regulations do not apply to contractual terms which reflect (a) mandatory statutory or regulatory provisions...

Claimants may argue that an exemption clause reflects statutory provisions. Interestingly, the wording of Regulation 4(2)(a) differs from the wording of the Schedule 1(e) of the 1994 Regulations in that the word "mandatory" has been added in the 1999 Regulations. The word "mandatory" appears in the Council Directive 93/13 on which the Regulations are modelled. Defendants may argue strongly that, whilst an exemption clause may reflect statutory provisions, they are not mandatory.

Further, Regulation 6(2) provides that:

> in so far as it is in plain intelligible language, the assessment of fairness of a term shall not relate:
>
> a) to the definition of the main subject matter of the contract, or
>
> b) to the adequacy of the price or remuneration, as against the goods or services supplied in exchange.

This is generally thought to exclude certain terms from the requirement of fairness. Those terms excluded are the core terms of the contract. Thus the courts must distinguish between those terms which express the substance of the bargain and those other incidental terms which surround them. The reason for the distinction is that the 1999 Regulations are not a mechanism of price control or indeed quality control. They are not intended to undermine the parties' freedom to contract.

It is interesting that in *Director General of Fair Trading* v *First National Bank Plc* [2002] 1 AC 481, the House of Lords took a restrictive interpretation of which terms count as core terms. Although this case in fact related to the 1994 Regulations, it is submitted that the reasoning of the House of Lords remains relevant to the 1999 Regulations. Lord Bingham said at paragraph 12:

> The object of the Regulations and the Directive is to protect consumers against the inclusion of unfair and prejudicial terms in standard-form contracts into which they enter, and that object would plainly be frustrated if regulation 3(2)(b) were so broadly interpreted as to cover any terms other than those falling squarely within it.

This suggests that Claimants are likely to find it difficult to argue that a term challenged by the Defendants falls within Regulation 6(2). Nevertheless Regulation 6(2) would appear to prevent Defendants from arguing that the rate of hire was itself unfair. The rate of hire is likely to be regarded as a core term.

Is the Term Unfair?

Regulation 5(1) provides that "a contractual term which has not been individually negotiated shall be regarded as unfair if, contrary to the requirement of good faith, it causes a significant imbalance in the parties' rights and obligations arising under the contract, to the detriment of the consumer".

Regulation 6(1) states that all the circumstances surrounding the contract must be taken into account when assessing whether a term is fair. In particular the courts are enjoined to consider the nature of the good or services concerned and the circumstances attending the conclusion of the contract.

Regard should also be had to Schedule 2 which lays down an "indicative and non-exhaustive list of terms which may be regarded as unfair". One example of this is a term which irrevocably binds the consumer to a term with which he had no real opportunity of becoming acquainted before the conclusion of the contract (schedule 2(1)(i) of the Regulations).

In *Director General of Fair Trading* v *First National Bank PLC* the House of Lords considered the meaning of the test for unfairness for the first time. It is worth setting out some passages from their speeches:

> A term falling within the scope of the Regulations is unfair if it causes a significant imbalance in the parties' rights and obligations under the contract to the detriment of the consumer in a manner or to an extent which is contrary to the requirement of good faith. The requirement of significant imbalance is met if a term is so weighted in favour of the supplier as to tilt the parties' rights and obligations under the contract significantly in his favour. This may be by the granting to the supplier of a beneficial option or discretion or power, or by the imposing on the consumer of a disadvantageous burden or risk or duty... The requirement of good faith in this context is one of fair and open dealing. Openness requires that the terms should be expressed fully, clearly and legibly, containing no concealed pitfalls or traps. Appropriate prominence should be given to terms which might operate disadvantageously to the customer. Fair dealing requires that a supplier should not, whether deliberately or unconsciously, take advantage of the consumer's necessity, indigence, lack of experience, unfamiliarity with the subject matter of the contract, weak bargaining position or any other factor listed in or analogous to those listed in Schedule 2 to the Regulations. Good faith in this context is not an artificial or technical concept; nor, since Lord Mansfield was its champion, is it a concept wholly unfamiliar to British lawyers. It looks to good standards of commercial morality and practice. Regulation 4(1) lays down a composite test, covering both the making and the substance of the contract, and must be applied bearing

clearly in mind the objective which the Regulations are designed to promote.
Lord Bingham at paragraph 17.

A contractual term in a consumer contract is unfair if "contrary to the requirement of good faith [it] causes a significant imbalance in the parties' rights and obligations under the contract to the detriment of the consumer". There can be no one single test of this. It is obviously useful to assess the impact of an impugned term on the parties' rights and obligations by comparing the effect of the contract with the term and the effect it would have without it. But the inquiry cannot stop there. It may also be necessary to consider the effect of the inclusion of the term on the substance or core of the transaction; whether if it were drawn to his attention the consumer would be likely to be surprised by it; whether the term is a standard term, not merely in similar non-negotiable consumer contracts, but in commercial contracts freely negotiated between parties acting on level terms and at arms' length; and whether, in such cases, the party adversely affected by the inclusion of the term or his lawyer might reasonably be expected to object to its inclusion and press for its deletion. The list is not necessarily exhaustive; other approaches may sometimes be more appropriate.
Lord Millett at paragraph 54.

Ultimately the question of whether or not a term is unfair is dependant on all the facts and circumstances of an individual case.

The Effect of a Clause being held to be "Unfair"
If a clause is found to be unfair it does not bind the consumer (Regulation 8(1)). Thus if the Defendant successfully argued that a term exempting a contract from Consumer Credit legislation was unfair, the Defendant could go on to argue that the provisions of the Consumer Credit Act ought to apply in the normal way. This may lead to the contract being unenforceable. To pursue such an attack, the Defendant is likely to need to join the credit hire company into the litigation to determine the specific issue of unfairness.

Sham / Pretence
Defendant insurers have attempted to argue that the twelve month extension clauses were a sham or a pretence. Very often cases came to court in which twelve months had already elapsed and the hire company had taken no steps to enforce the agreement. The issue came before the Court of Appeal in the conjoined appeals under the name *Burdis* v *Livsey* [2003] QB 36.

The Court of Appeal first considered the narrow definition of sham propounded by Lord Justice Diplock (as he then was) in *Snook* v *West Riding Investments Ltd* [1967] 2 QB 786, 802:

for acts or documents to be a sham...all the parties thereto must have a common intention that the acts or documents are not to create the legal rights and obligations which they give the appearance of creating.

The weakness in this argument was that in credit hire cases, there is rarely, if at all, any evidence of deceit or improper motive on the part of the Claimant. The Court of Appeal were content to quote from the judgment below of Judge Harris QC in the Oxford County Court:

There was no suggestion in last year's cases and there is none in the instant ones, that any of the claimants who entered into their credit or insurance agreements had any improper motive whatsoever. They merely and perfectly legitimately wanted their cars mending and a substitute providing without significant expense to themselves. There is no evidence that they had any intention to avoid, legitimately or illegitimately, the application of the consumer credit legislation.

Thus the agreements could not be shams in that narrow sense. However the courts remain alert to agreements that are shams in the wider sense that the agreements do not do what they say on the packet. For example in *Antoniades* v *Villiers* [1990] 1 AC 417 the House of Lords refused to give effect to an agreement which called itself a licence and reserved a right of occupation to the landlord. The reserved right was never intended to be exercised. It was a pretence to avoid the provisions of the Rent Acts. A similar result was reached in *Gisborne* v *Burton* [1989] 1 QB 390, where the landlord had tried to evade the Agricultural Holdings Act 1948.

In *Burdis* the Court of Appeal noted that "in this type of case the courts have made it clear that they will look at the scheme as a whole if there is more than one transaction and subsequent conduct in order to determine its effect and validity."

They continued at paragraph 33:

In the instant case the court is concerned with consumer protection legislation. It is not possible to contract out of the provisions which regulate some transactions but the Act says that other transactions are exempt. There is therefore nothing wrong with entering or attempting to enter into such a transaction. Either it is exempt or it is regulated and the courts must decide which.

The point was that the court simply had to decide whether the agreement in question meets the requirements of an exempt agreement or not. Guidance was taken from Lord Hoffman's words in *Norglen Ltd* v *Reeds Rains Prudential Ltd* [1999] 2 AC 1:

The question is simply whether upon its true construction, the statute applies to the transaction. Tax avoidance schemes are perhaps the best example. They either work ... or they do not.... If they do not work, the reason.... is simply that upon the true construction of the statute, the transaction which was designed to avoid the charge to tax actually comes within it. It is not that the statute has a penumbral spirit which strikes down devices or stratagems designed to avoid its terms or exploit its loopholes.

The court considered that on their face the credit hire agreements were exempt from the Act. The Defendant argued that the court should infer that there was no limit to the credit period because the insurance arrangement was a pretence and was not pursued by the hire company in practice. This failed on the facts. Judge Harris QC had found that there were payments from the insurer to the hire company which had the effect of discharging the Claimants' debts. The source of the insurer's funds was irrelevant. There is nothing unusual about the circular flow of funds around a group of companies. Accordingly the Court of Appeal upheld the Judge's decision that there was no sham or pretence on these facts. For completeness, we quote from paragraphs 39 and 44 of the judgment:

These points [relating to the insurance arrangements] were obviously considered by the judge who, as we have said, referred to the scheme as a whole as being sloppily executed and to the insurance arrangement as being artificial. But the documents do show an intention to create genuine insurance arrangements. The underwriting agreement contains many of the terms one would expect to find in such an agreement and there was an assumption of risk by underwriters. Subject to the point about the policy wording, which was obviously a mistake, a claimant would have a valid claim under the policy for the cost of hire and repairs if no payment was made by Angel. In effect the risk assumed by underwriters was of the solvency of the Helphire Group. There is nothing wrong or unusual with insurance arrangements which have this effect...

We have so far considered the insurers' main attack on the scheme. The fact that customers who did not claim on the insurance were not pursued was not considered in any detail by the Judge. But just because the scheme was, as he said, "sloppily enforced" does not lead to the conclusion that the credit hire and repair agreements were intended to have some meaning contrary to their express terms. Commercial parties may, and often do, choose not to enforce their strict legal rights without intending to create or demonstrate some different state of affairs. Other matters relied on by the insurers about the way in which the Helphire scheme was run do not in our judgment advance their case. Looked at from the claimants' point of view there was no pretence. They got exactly what they bargained for: car repair and hire at little or no cost. It might be said that it is only the insurers' attack on these schemes which has raised the spectre of long term credit because in the ordinary way claims of this kind are settled within weeks of the accident.

This does not necessarily mean that the issue of pretence / sham is dead. The decision was based on factual findings about how the particular companies and their contracts operated. There may be room for Defendant insurers to argue sham / pretence if on the facts of a different scheme, with a different contractual or corporate set up, no payments are being made by the nominal insurer.

In *Corbett* v *Gaskin* (31 August 2007 unreported) HHJ Harris QC had to consider a challenge to a different credit hire agreement. He identified a number of curious features of the agreement, including that: two of the three companies referred to on the face of the contract either did not exist or were dormant; despite the wording of the contract, the Claimant had never been asked to pay hire charges and insurance cover was never arranged under the terms of the contract, although other cover was provided. The court criticised these arrangement as "complex and misleading". However he rejected the Defendant's argument that the contract was a sham or a pretence, saying that the main object of the agreement was the provision of a car to the Claimant, probably at no cost to himself, and none of the other clauses were repugnant to this purpose. A similar result was reached in *Barker* v *First West Yorkshire Limited* (13 September 2007 unreported).

Chapter 4

RESIDUAL LIABILITY FOR HIRE IN RELATION TO CONSUMER CREDIT

The issue here can be stated shortly. The Claimant in *Dimond* v *Lovell* argued that it did not matter whether the credit hire agreement between the Claimant and the hire company was unenforceable. The Claimant's car had still been damaged in an accident that was the Defendant's fault. The Claimant was, they argued, still entitled to damages for loss of use.

This issue is of significance to the issue of damages generally. To what extent should collateral benefits received after the accident be deducted from the claim? How far should courts go behind an agreement which forms the basis of a claim?

The Court Of Appeal

In the Court of Appeal, the Claimant in *Dimond* v *Lovell* argued that the Claimant was deprived of the loss of use of her car for eight days. Further, Scott V–C stated (at paragraph 74) that there was no doubt that she had a genuine need for a replacement vehicle and that the reasonable cost to her of obtaining one would have been recoverable as damages. On the other hand, he pointed out that in any event, she had had the use of a replacement vehicle and had no legal liability to pay for it. Further, this came about not through the benevolence of a friend or relation but because 1st Automotive's car hiring agreement had fallen foul of the Act. If she could nevertheless recover damages, she had said that she would pay the damages over to 1st Automotive even though she had no legal liability to do so.

The Claimant relied upon *Donnelly* v *Joyce* [1974] 1 QB 454 in which a Claimant was awarded a sum to compensate for the care his mother had given him. In particular, she relied upon a very wide *dicta* by Megaw LJ which appeared to extend this principle of third party recovery beyond voluntary care. The other case invoked was *McAll* v *Brooks* (1984) RTR 99 which relied upon the *dicta* of Megaw LJ in Donnelly v Joyce to extend the principle of third party recovery to a Claimant who was claiming hire charges from a Defendant even though the hire charges were not recoverable from the Claimant since the hirers were providing the car under an insurance policy and they were not licensed to carry on an insurance business.

The Defendant emphasised the general rule that in tort, damages are merely compensatory and that for whatever reason, the Claimant simply had not suffered a loss with regard to using a car. In particular, the Defendant relied upon the case of *Hunt* v *Severs* [1994] 2 AC 350 in which the House of Lords, through the speech of Lord Bridge which was agreed by the other Law Lords, restricted the voluntary care cases and in particular disapproved Megaw LJ's *dicta* in *Donnelly* v *Joyce*.

Further, and perhaps most significantly, Lord Bridge and therefore the House of Lords adopted the view expressed by Lord Denning in *Cunningham* v *Harrison* [1973] QB 942 that "in England the injured plaintiff who recovers damages under this head should hold them on trust for the voluntary carer".

At paragraph 88 of *Dimond* v *Lovell*, Scott V–C stated:

> Lord Bridge's reasoning, in disapproving the reasoning of Megaw LJ in Donnelly v Joyce, fatally undermines, in my judgment, *McAll* v *Brooks*. If a plaintiff has received a benefit from a third party that has, in the event, met his need with no cost to himself, be it a need for care services or a need for a replacement vehicle, the court may allow an award of damages in order to enable the plaintiff to recompense the third party. The plaintiff will then hold the amount of the award in trust for the third party. But if the circumstances of the case do not permit a trust for the third party to be imposed on the damages, the plaintiff cannot recover the damages. He does not need to recover damages in order to meet his own losses for, in the event, he suffered none. To allow him to recover in circumstances where the trust solution could not be applied would lead to a recovery by the plaintiff of more than he had lost. These, in my judgment, are the principles to be applied in the present case.

At paragraph 89, Scott V–C analysed whether the circumstances of the case merited the imposition of a trust in favour of 1st Automotive:

> Mrs Dimond's need for a replacement vehicle was met by 1st Automotive. They supplied her with a vehicle under the terms of the hiring agreement that she signed. But the agreement is unenforceable for 1st Automotive's failure to comply with the requirements of the 1974 Act. 1st Automotive certainly did not provide the vehicle out of benevolence. It supplied the vehicle in the course of its business. Would the law in those circumstances impose a trust on the damages in favour of 1st Automotive? In my judgment, certainly not. The statutory requirements of which 1st Automotive were in breach were imposed by Parliament and. under

subordinate legislation, by the Secretary of State. I can see no reason at all how it can be right for equity, via the medium of a trust, to remedy 1st Automotive's failure to comply with the statutory requirements.

He then gave the example of the case of *Orakpo* v *Manson Investments Ltd* [1978] AC 95 and went on (at paragraphs 90–91):

> In the present case, the 1974 Act has enacted that an agreement not "properly executed" is unenforceable. It is not, in my judgment, the function of the courts to remedy that enforceability by creating a trust in favour of 1st Automotive over damages payable to Mrs Dimond. If *McAll* v *Brooks* had been decided after Hunt v Severs the same reasoning would, in my view, have prevented recovery in that case. A trust in favour of the insurance company that had been carrying on an illegal insurance business created in order to remedy the consequences of illegality would in my view, have been wrong in principle. If a trust of the damages in favour of the supplier of the replacement vehicle cannot be created, Hunt v Severs stands, in my judgment, as an authority that bars recovery of the damages from the defendant.

> In my judgment, in disagreement with the Recorder, *McAll* v *Brooks* is no longer good law and Mrs Dimond who has fortuitously obtained a replacement vehicle without having to pay for it, cannot recover as damages the amount she would have had to pay if her agreement with 1st Automotive had been enforceable.

The House of Lords

In the House of Lords, the arguments were put slightly differently with an emphasis on restitution backed up by the reiteration of the principle of *res inter alios acta.*

Unjust enrichment

The judgments
The Appellant argued that if the hiring agreement was unenforceable then Mrs Dimond would have been unjustly enriched.

Lord Hoffman (at page 11) addressed this point robustly:

> The real difficulty, as it seems to me, is that to treat Mrs. Dimond as having been unjustly enriched would be inconsistent with the purpose of section 61(1). Parliament intended that if a consumer credit agreement was improperly executed, then subject to the enforcement powers of the court, the debtor should not have to pay. This meant that Parliament contemplated that he might be enriched and I do not see how it is open to the court to say

that this consequence is unjust and should be reversed by a remedy at common law: compare *Orakpo* v. *Manson Investments Ltd.* [1978] A.C. 95.

Lord Hobhouse (at page 21) was even more brief:

> Again I agree with your Lordships that there is no basis for implying an obligation of the hirer to pay contrary to the statute. Nor is there any basis for the application of some restitutionary principle.

However, as part of his reasoning he also mentioned:

> The contemplation of the parties was that the hirer should not in fact pay out of her own pocket for the hiring of the car. In the present case she has not been unjustly enriched; her position is precisely that which was intended.

Again, this potentially leaves open room for attempts at distinguishing the judgment in those cases where the contemplation of the parties was that the hirer should in fact pay out of her own pocket in the event of non-recovery from the negligent third party.

However, Defendants could rely not only on the other comments of both Lords Hoffman and Hobhouse but also on the wider policy issues of the Act. It is worth looking at the basis of the arguments before the House of Lords since they may well arise again with regard to other aspects of credit hire such as the common law arguments.

The academic justification
The Claimant founded her claim upon *Pavey and Matthews Pty Limited* v *Paul* [1987] 162 CLR 221 and *Deglman* v *Guaranty Trust Co. of Canada* [1954] 3 DLR 785.

Both cases involved an analysis by the Court of the statutory purpose of the relevant enactment. In both cases the Court held that the purpose of the statute was not undermined by granting recovery. The House of Lords did not find that this applies to the 1974 Act's scheme.

The Builders Licensing Act 1971 under question had no similar provision for differential remedies in the event of a breach rendering the contract unenforceable as with the Consumer Credit Act. Furthermore s.9(6), which barred a remedy in certain circumstances, did not apply to the breach in question. This would have therefore distinguished the Australian scheme from the provisions of the 1974 Act.

In *Deglman* at 788 Rand J. stated that the statute "...did not touch the principle of restitution?". However, it was pointed out that the decision did not appear to have been extended in Canada to licensing cases of that nature: see *Calax Construction* v *Lepofsky* [1974] 50 DLR 69.

Similarly, the American Courts had rejected the claims of those seeking a *quantum meruit* for work done without an appropriate licence: see *Hale* v *Kreisel* [1927] 215 NWR 227 at 228-229 and *Louisville Trust Company* v *Monsky* [1969] Ky., 444 SW 2d 120 at 121-122.

The Defendant argued that even if Pavey was correctly decided, it was not authority for the extension of the principle to the Consumer Credit Act.

In particular, it was emphasised that failure to recover would be due to a failure to comply with statutory obligations. Even then, the contract would not be wholly unenforceable, but only unenforceable by the hire company. See *Geraghty* v *Awwad* (C.A. 25th November 1999 - unreported) at Part VIII "*Quantum Meruit*", page 23.

The Defendant also averred that the law of England never permits a party to take advantage of his own default or wrong: see generally *Alghussein Establishment* v *Eton College* [1988] 1 WLR 587 at 591D-594D. This was all the more so when there has been a breach of statutory requirements. See *Boston Deep Sea Fishing Co* v *Ansell* [1888] 39 Ch.D. 339 at 364-365; *Sumpter* v *Hedges* [1898] 1 QB 673 at 674 and 675-7; *Parkinson* v *College of Ambulance Limited* [1925] 2 KB 1 at 15-16; *Berg* v *Sadler and Moore* [1937] 2 KB 158 at 163, 166 and 168-9 and *Bolton* v *Mahadeva* [1972] 1 WLR 1009 at 1011H-1012B and 1014B-C.

As Millet LJ stated in *Ingram* v *I.R.C.* [1997] 4 All ER 395 at p. 417j:

> If Parliament has drawn a line in a particular place, however incongruously, it is not for the Courts to draw it elsewhere.

The Act is based upon the findings of the Crowther Report and demonstrates the coherent structure of remedies recommended by it. The Report made it plain that there should be a division between those breaches which would permit some form of remedy and those breaches which were to be treated as requiring the contract to be unenforceable against the debtor. See paragraphs 4.2.13-15; 6.1.15-16; 6.5.3; 6.11.1-6.11.10 of the Report. The 1974 Act followed that approach, particularly in section 127.

In *Pavey and Matthews* v *Paul* at page 243, all members of the majority expressly stated that their decision did not affect the validity of cases refusing alternative recovery via unjust enrichment where the agreement was unenforceable under the Moneylenders Act: see pages 229-230, 261-262 and the final paragraph at page 270 (although it should be noted that Brennan J made a strong dissenting judgment. See also *Deposit & Investment Co. Ltd* v *Kaye* [1963] NSWR 833 at 837-8 and 840-845.

The Moneylenders Acts were well known as treating "unenforceable" to mean no alternative remedy: see *Kasumu* v *Baba-Egbe* [1956] AC 539 at 551-2. Defendants may argue using the House of Lords speeches in *Dimond* that the same approach should be made to the Act. In particular, the Act replaced the Moneylenders Acts which themselves referred to "unenforceable" agreements. In *Orakpo* v *Manson Investments* [1978] AC 95, the House of Lords examined the question of unenforceability under the Moneylenders Acts. In that case, an otherwise meritorious moneylender was refused a restitutionary remedy on the basis that recovery would frustrate the purpose of the statute.

The decision in *Orakpo* was cited, without criticism, as an example of public policy denying a restitutionary remedy in *Banque Financière de la Cité* v *Parc (Battersea) Limited* at 234D.

Further, paragraphs 6.11.5 and 6.11.10 of the Crowther Report indicate that the fact that consumers might have windfalls by having possession of goods without payment was known to the Committee, yet restitution was not specifically mentioned.

Res inter alios acta
(literally, thing done among others)
The second line of the Claimant's argument in this regard was to argue that it did not matter whether she was liable to pay for the hire.

Lord Hoffman stated (at page 12) that, "This argument has very respectable support in the authorities" and he went on to mention *Parry* v *Cleaver* [1970] AC 1, *Donnelly* v *Joyce* [1974] QB 454 and *McAll* v *Brooks* [1984] RTR 99. Having quoted from *McAll*, he went on:

> That is the high water mark of authority in favour of 1st Automotive. But since high water the tide has retreated. The courts have realised that a general principle of *res inter alios acta* which assumes that damages will be paid by "the wrongdoer" out of his own pocket is not in accordance with reality. The truth is that virtually all compensation is paid directly out of public or insurance funds and that through these channels the burden of compensation is spread across the whole community through an intricate series of economic links. Often, therefore, the sources of "third party benefits" will not in reality be third parties at all. Their cost will also be

borne by the community through taxation or increased prices for goods and services.

He then quoted Lord Bridge in *Hunt* v *Severs* [1994] 2 AC 350 as Scott V-C had done in the Court of Appeal and also referred to the fact that for voluntary carers the Claimant "can sue only if he claims as trustee for the person who provided the services". He then concluded:

> This case is of course far away from the gratuitous provision of services (usually by a relative) which was considered suitable for recovery as trustee in *Hunt* v. *Severs* [1994] 2 A.C. 350. If Mrs. Dimond is allowed to sue Mr. Lovell as trustee for 1st Automotive, the effect will be to confer legal rights upon 1st Automotive by virtue of an agreement which the Act of 1974 has declared to be unenforceable. This would be contrary to the intention of the Act. The only way, therefore, in which Mrs. Dimond could recover damages for the notional cost of hiring a car which she has actually had for free is if your Lordships were willing to create another exception to the rule against double recovery. I can see no basis for doing so. The policy of the Act of 1974 is to penalise 1st Automotive for not entering into a properly executed agreement. A consequence is often to confer a benefit upon the debtor, but that is a consequence rather than the primary purpose. There is no reason of policy why the law should insist that Mrs. Dimond should be able to retain that benefit and make a double recovery rather than that it should reduce the liability of Mr. Lovell's insurers.

Lord Hobhouse made a careful analysis of the basis for loss of use claims and in particular for the claim for hire and stated that whilst "Each case depends upon its own facts", "loss of use of the chattel in question is, in principle, a loss for which compensation should be paid". However, he went on:

> one of the relevant principles is that compensation is not paid for an avoided loss. So, if the plaintiff has been able to avoid suffering a particular head of loss by a process which is not too remote (as is insurance), the plaintiff will not be entitled to recover in respect of that avoided loss.

It should be noted that the approaches of Lords Hoffman and Hobhouse have subtle differences. Lord Hoffman put emphasis on the breach of the statute and the fact that this should not be remedied by the common law. Lord Hobhouse's approach was broader and simply emphasised the principle of compensatory loss coupled with remoteness.

This difference may become important if a case involved a hire agreement which was unenforceable for reasons other than breach of an absolute provision of the Act. Lord Hoffman's approach may potentially offer some hope to Claimants in trying to distinguish the case although given his general approach to the question it remains to be seen what success such an argument would have.

If the issue does arise in other contexts, Defendants may also rely upon the case of *Hardwick* v *Hudson* [1999] 1 WLR 1770 at pages 1776A-F and 1777A-G. Further, the Law Commission Report No.262 Damages for Personal Injury: Medical, Nursing and Other Expenses: Collateral Benefits paragraphs 3.44-3.66 examined *Hunt* v *Severs*. Whilst it recommended reversal of the actual decision in that case, so that damages would be awarded even though the gratuitous carer was the tortfeasor, it was strongly of the view that the general approach of the House of Lords: (that the loss was suffered by the third party carer and not by the claimant and that the claimant was therefore under a legal duty to pay over damages for past care to the carer) was correct. It decisively rejected Donnelly v Joyce at paragraphs 3.46-3.47. The Law Commission's review of collateral benefits has concluded that there should be no change in the present law: see paragraphs 9.8-9.9; 11.18-11.22 and 11.53.

Burdis v Livsey

The Claimant in *Burdis* v *Livsey* put the argument slightly differently. He argued that an improperly executed regulated agreement still gives rise to contractual obligations. The only effect of the Consumer Credit Act is to prevent the hirer enforcing his rights. It was argued that in these circumstances, there was nothing in principle wrong with the claimants recovering the cost of discharging their obligations under the contract. The Claimant also offered an undertaking that they would pay over to the hire company whatever was recovered in damages.

The Court of Appeal was unimpressed, saying at paragraph 58:

> We think the short answer to these submissions is that double recovery is a bar to the analysis and it is not overcome by the undertaking. Even though the contractual obligations of the claimant to pay Helphire for hire and repairs subsist if the credit agreements are unenforceable Helphire have no enforceable right to recover these amounts. The claimant has not paid and cannot be required to pay them so that if he recovers from the defendant there will be double recovery. The undertaking given to the court is truly collateral and could not be said to be the consequence of the defendant's tort. It is to be noted that the Court of Appeal was not tempted by a similar undertaking offered in *Dimond*

In *Bee* v *Jenson* [2007] EWCA Civ 923, in a case on insurance law and damages, Longmore LJ commented that:

if he [the Claimant] has in fact reasonably made arrangements for a hire car, there is no reason why he should not recover the cost of hire, whether or not he has rendered himself liable for the hire charges...in so doing he may in legal jargon be recovering general damages rather than special damages.

Claimants may seek to use this *dicta* to argue that the Defendant should still have to pay for car hire, even where the agreement is unenforceable. Defendant may argue that this was not the precise point in issue in that case, since it was not a credit hire case: the hire was arranged through insurance. Furthermore, Longmore LJ specifically referred to and approved *Dimond v Lovell* [2002] 1 AC 1067 in which the House of Lords held that the Claimant could not recover credit hire charges where the agreement was unenforceable under the Consumer Credit Act 1974.

Chapter 5

CONSUMER CREDIT ACT 2006

The Consumer Credit Act 2006 introduces a range of legislative reforms. It was felt that the 1974 Act had not proved consumers with sufficient protection. The reforming zeal can be seen in the Department of Trade and Industry press release 30 March 2006 which states "Millions of consumers will enjoy greater protection from unscrupulous lenders".

Practitioners need to be aware that there is a complicated timetable for the implementation of the 2006 Act. Different parts of the Act are due to become law at different times. Care is needed whether particular parts of the Act are in force at any given time.

This book is not the place to provide a detailed commentary on the entire scheme of the 2006 Act. Not all the reforms are relevant to the field of credit hire. We defer to specialist works for this (in particular Goode's Consumer Credit Law and Practice).

Instead, this chapter lists the main changes and then focuses on three issues. First, the change in definition of regulated agreements. Second, the repeal of the provision making improperly executed agreements automatically unenforceable. Third, the new concept of "unfair relationships".

Main Changes

The following bullet points aim to provide a summary of some of the main changes introduced by the 2006 Act. They are not exhaustive.

- Introduction of wider ranging requirement for companies offering credit to be licensed.
- More extensive duty on the Office of Fair Trading to monitor companies together with more extensive enforcement powers such as improved powers of entry and search.
- New independent Consumer Credit Appeals Tribunal to hear appeals from decisions of the Office of Fair Trading.

- Alternative Dispute Resolution Service through the Financial Services Ombudsman Scheme.
- Further protection of consumers through, *inter alia*, notices on arrears, no compound interest and provision of periodic statements.

Change in Definition of Regulated Agreements

One of the major reforms in the new legislation is the removal of the existing £25,000 financial limit on regulated consumer credit agreements. This is to be achieved by simply deleting the old section 8(2).

This means that every credit agreement where the debtor is an individual (defined in section 189(1)) will be a regulated agreement unless it is exempt.

This amendment is timetabled to come into force on 6 April 2008.

Enforceability of Agreements

The position under the 1974 Act was that an improperly executed regulated agreement (i.e. one that did not comply with the requirements of the Act) could not be enforced by the creditor without an order of the court (section 65(1)). Section 127(3) and (4) specify situations in which the court is prevented from granting such an order: this effectively renders the agreements automatically unenforceable.

The problem with this state of affairs was that it appeared unfair to the creditor to render an agreement automatically unenforceable where the defect may not have caused any prejudice to the debtor.

The 2006 Act deals with this problem by repealing s127(3) and (4). This leaves it entirely to the court's discretion whether or not to grant an enforcement order. This repeal occurred on 6 April 2007.

The test will now be as laid down in section 127(1):

> the court shall dismiss the application [for an enforcement order] if, but only if, it considers it just to do so having regard to (i) prejudice caused to any person by the contravention in question, and the degree of culpability for it...

In considering whether to grant the enforcement order the court may "reduce or discharge" any part of the sum payable to compensate for prejudice suffered by the debtor (section 127(2)). Further the court retains the powers in section 135 and 136 to make the enforcement order conditional, suspend the operation of any term of the order and amend any term of any agreement as a consequence of making the order.

This is important because the decision of the House of Lords in *Dimond* was based on the finding that the breaches of the 1974 Act rendered the agreement automatically unenforceable. It is not clear whether the same decision would have been reached if the agreement had merely been potentially unenforceable. This would leave it open for Claimants to argue that while the agreement only might be unenforceable there remains the chance that it could be enforced against them. The Defendant's response is to argue that agreements are either enforceable or unenforceable as a matter of fact. They cannot be half enforceable. The Defendant would have to invite the Judge to decide whether the particular agreement would be enforced or not.

Unfair Relationships

The existing arrangement for "extortionate credit bargains" in sections 137 – 140 of the 1974 Act were repealed on 6 April 2007. This is significant because in practice it was very difficult to establish that an agreement was extortionate.

The new section 140A will provide that:

> the court may make an order under section 140B in connection with a credit agreement if it determines that the relationship between the creditor and the debtor arising out of the agreement is unfair to the debtor because of one or more of the following:
>
> (a) any of the terms of the agreement and any related agreement;
> (b) the way in which the creditor has exercised or enforced any of his rights under the agreement or any related agreement;
> (c) any other thing done (or not done) by, or on behalf of, the creditor (either before or after the making of the agreement or any related agreement.

The court is enjoined to "have regard to all matters it thinks are relevant" in deciding whether a relationship is unfair (section 140A(2)).

It remains to be seen what sort of factors will persuade a court that a relationship is unfair. No further guidance is given in the statute. However it is suggested that the courts will draw guidance from the definition of unfair in the Unfair Terms in Consumer Contracts Regulations 1999.

Interestingly if a debtor alleges that a relationship is unfair, the burden of proof rests on the creditor to prove that it is not unfair by virtue of section 140B(9).

There are arguments that Defendants could advance in relation specifically to credit hire agreements. For example it is frequently the case that the Claimant has not read or had explained to them the terms of the agreement that they sign up to. All too often Claimants think, or are told, that the hire car is free. Might this render a relationship unfair? How about the degree of involvement of the hire company in the subsequent litigation?

If an agreement is found to be unfair, the court has wide ranging powers by section 140B to redress the unfairness. This includes the power to set aside any duties imposed on the debtor by the agreement (section 140B(1)(e)).

An interesting argument for Defendants is that section 140A applied simply to "credit agreements". This is important because other sections in the legislation refer to "regulated agreements".

The subtle point is that section 16 divides credit agreements into those which are regulated and those which are exempt. Most credit hire companies have managed to make their agreements exempt. However Defendants may potentially argue that by using the phrase credit agreement rather than regulated agreement, as used elsewhere in the statute, Parliament intends section 140A to apply to all credit agreements regardless of whether they are regulated or exempt.

This is a point which has not been argued in the courts. If a Defendant did wish to run such an argument, it would have to be properly and precisely pleaded.

The consequence if this argument succeeds is also unclear. *Dimond*, as noted above, only covered the situation where the agreement was automatically unenforceable. Claimants can argue that it just does not matter if an agreement is potentially unenforceable. They are after all not obliged to enter uncertain litigation in order to mitigate their loss. Defendants can argue that Judges should determine for themselves whether the relationship is unfair and what the consequence is. Agreements cannot be half unfair: they are either fair or unfair and it only waits for the court to determine which. Defendants running this argument may wish to consider whether to join the hire company as a party to the proceedings.

Chapter 6

OTHER POTENTIAL CREDIT ARGUMENTS

For a short period after *Dimond* v *Lovell*, both Claimants and Defendants ran a wide range of consumer credit arguments. The bulk of these arguments are no longer relevant in practice, either because a higher court decision has authoritatively ruled them out or because most credit hire agreements are now drafted to avoid any problems. The result is that it is no longer common to run consumer credit arguments in the County Courts. Consequently this chapter is rather shorter than in previous editions of this book.

There remain however a number of consumer credit issues which do continue to crop up. This chapter deals with the following:-

    1. Cancellable Agreements
    2. Agreements purporting to be Regulated
    3. Consumer Hire
    4. More than One Debtor / Hirer
    5. Distance Selling Regulations
    6. Prescribed Terms
    7. Human Rights Law
    8. Consent
    9. Spot Hire Agreements
    10. Individuals

1. Cancellable agreements

If the agreement is regulated, Defendants may argue that the agreement is a cancellable agreement as defined in section 67 of the Act, in particular:

A regulated agreement may be cancelled by the debtor or hirer in accordance with this Part if the antecedent negotiations included oral representations made when in the presence of the debtor or hirer by an individual acting as, or on behalf of, the negotiator, unless:

. . . . .

(b)   the unexecuted agreement is signed by the debtor or hirer at premises at which any of the following is carrying on business (whether on a permanent or temporary basis) –

(i) the creditor or owner;

(ii) any party to a linked transaction (other than the debtor or hirer or a relative of his);

(iii) the negotiator in any antecedent negotiations?

If an agreement is cancellable, section 64 sets out a duty to give notice of cancellation rights. The significance of this is that it carries the same peremptory significance as prescribed terms since section 127(4)(b) states that, the court shall not make an enforcement order under section 65(1) in the case of a cancellable agreement if section 64(1) was not complied with.

Defendants would be well-advised to argue this in particular when contracts appear to have had the price and an estimate for the period of hire inserted at the time of the making of the agreement.

Credit hire companies may be able to argue that there were no antecedent negotiations or oral representations or that any that were made were not by their servants or agents. Further, that the contract was signed at their premises and complied with the other requirements of section 67(b).

In *Aggett* v *Aston Rothbury Factors Limited*, HHJ Overend, Exeter County Court, 6 July 2001, HHJ Overend stated in this regard:

> In my judgment it cannot be said that the mere indication that terms or conditions may be found on the back of the form, amount to "antecedent negotiations". Support for this approach is to be found in the decision of *Moorgate Property Services Limited* v *Kabir* [1995] CCLR 74, in respect of which a note appears in Professor Goode's Consumer Credit Practice under section 56 in the following terms:
>
> > "Concerned that if almost anything said to the dealer were to be treated as "included" in the antecedent negotiations, the Court of Appeal, and in particular Staughton LJ, introduced a test of "materiality". The mere statement that "further financial particulars would have to be sought from the creditor" failed this test"
>
> Accordingly I conclude that neither agreement was a cancellable agreement.

It should be noted that there are numerous Regulations concerning cancellation rights. For example: the Consumer Credit (Cancellation Notices and Copies of Documents) Regulations 1983; The Consumer Credit (Notice of Cancellation Rights) (Exemptions) Regulations 1983; The Consumer Credit (Repayment of Credit on Cancellation) Regulations 1983; The Consumer Protection (Cancellation of Contracts Concluded away from Business Premises) Regulations 1987; and the Consumer Credit (Agreements and Cancellation Notices and Copies of Documents) (Amendment) Regulations 1988.

2. Agreements purporting to be regulated

If an agreement is regulated it is very difficult to fully comply with all of the prescribed forms and terms as set out in the Act and the Regulations. Not only do the Consumer Credit (Agreement) Regulations 1983 apply but also potentially numerous others including the Consumer Credit (Total Charge for Credit) Regulations 1980 and the Consumer Credit (Rebate on Early Settlement) Regulations 1983. If the agreement is cancellable, not only may cancellation notices be required but cooling-off periods, for example, may also be necessary.

Defendants and Claimants should be aware of these details when dealing with agreements which purport to be regulated.

An interesting argument in this regard involves what exactly is to be covered in the total charge for credit.

Paragraph 9 of Schedule 1 of the 1983 Regulations provides that a regulated agreement must state the total charge for credit. These are defined in the Consumer Credit (Total Charge for Credit) Regulations 1980. Effectively, this is part of the prescribed form (for which, see below).

Whilst at present the argument would be speculative, it might be possible to argue that the difference between spot hire and credit hire charges, in other words any uplift, amounts to the total charge for credit. Potentially, this may not have been included even within an agreement purporting to be regulated.

This would be helped by the comments of the House of Lords in *Dimond* who analysed the credit hire charges and concluded that they must include an uplift for the extra services provided. Lord Hoffman, for example, stated, "By virtue of [Mrs Dimond's] contract, she obtained not only the use of the car but additional benefits as well."

The argument also appears to be supported by Regulation 5(1)(c) of the Consumer Credit (Total Charge for Credit) Regulations 1980. It specifically excludes from the total charge for credit any charge which would be payable if the transaction were for cash. Effectively, it may be argued, this would be the equivalent "spot hire" amount, in other words the charge if credit had not been provided.

The cases of *Huntpast Limited* v *Leadbetter & Ors* [1993] CCLR 15 and *Wilson* v *First County Trust* [2001] 2 WLR 302; [2000] Times 6 December are useful with regard to what items are to be included in the total charge for credit.

3. Consumer hire: section 15

The Exemption Order does not exempt regulated consumer hire agreements. Therefore where agreements are capable of subsisting for more than three months this remains open as an area of attack for Defendants. If the period of hire lasts for more than that period any such arguments will be strengthened.

In this regard, it may be the case that a number of different agreements have been entered into for which the total number of days of hire is more than three months. Defendants may want to argue that in substance the agreements were in fact one single agreement which was capable of lasting for more than three months. The case of *Story and Pallister* v *National Westminster Bank* [1999] Lloyd's Rep. Bank. 261; [1999] C.C.L.R. 70; [1999] Times 14 May; [1999] 6 CL 289 (in the context of multiple agreements) provides some support for such an approach.

As mentioned earlier, the technical argument suggesting that the three months in fact relates to the period of the agreement and not to the period of the hire remains although in the light of the Court of Appeal's judgment in *Dimond* v *Lovell* may be unlikely to have much success.

In *Aggett* v *Aston Rothbury Factors Limited*, HHJ Overend, Exeter County Court, 6 July 2001, HHJ Overend accepted the submission that the period of three months applied to the period of the agreement as a whole and not just to the hire period. He stated that:

> In my judgment, although initially attracted by the argument that the three months period related solely to the bailment, I am persuaded by Mr Hammill that his submissions are correct for the reasons he outlined.

However, this point was argued in *Clark* v *Ardington Electrical Services and others*, HHJ Harris, Oxford County Court, 14 September 2001. HHJ Harris quoted the Vice Chancellor in *Dimond* and also from Professor Goode's work. He then went on:

> Confronted with concurring opinions from the Vice Chancellor, who even without the benefit of submissions, was certainly considering the point, and from an authority whom the Vice Chancellor has called when disagreeing with him on another topic an "acknowledged master of the intricacies of consumer credit control", I think it would be inappropriate for me at this level to differ from them both. I therefore follow and apply what Sir Richard Scott said. I find that these agreements are not consumer hire agreements within section 15 of that Act.

The point was argued again before the Court of Appeal in *Burdis* v *Livsey*. The insurers' argument failed, with the Court holding at paragraphs 48-9:

> Although sub-section (1)(b) could have been more clearly drafted we agree with the judge's construction. Section 15 is directed at the long-term bailment of goods which are not the subject of hire purchase agreements. Sub-section (1)(b) is intended to refer to the period of such bailment and not to any other obligations which might be assumed under the agreement. Sub-section (1)(c) is merely intended to limit the application of the section to agreements of a certain size. It does not extend the type of agreement to which the section is intended to refer.

> Some support for this construction can be derived from the surrounding sections of the Act. Section 15 appears as one of six sections which closely define different categories of regulated agreements. Section 18 to which we will return contemplates that one must look at any agreement to see whether any part of it falls within one of these defined categories, in which case that part must be treated separately. This suggests that the intention was to confine the different categories of agreement. The construction contended for by the insurers gives a much wider definition of a consumer hire agreement than we think Parliament intended.

4. More than one debtor or hirer

Section 185 of the Act provides that where an actual or prospective agreement has two or more debtors or hirers (not being a partnership or other unincorporated body of persons), anything required to be done under the Act in relation to one of them is required for all of them.

However, anything done under the Act by any one of them shall have effect for all of them.

5. Distance Selling Regulations

Depending on the facts, Defendants may be able to argue the hire company has not complied with the Consumer Protection (Distance Selling) Regulations 2000 (SI 2000/2334). These Regulations apply to contracts formed exclusively over the telephone or by e-mail.

The most important Regulations are:

- Regulation 7 which requires the supplier to provide the consumer with specified information prior to the conclusion of the contract. This includes information on the right to cancel the contract.
- Regulation 8 which requires the supplier to confirm information given over the telephone in writing and to offer additional information including the terms and conditions and procedure in relation to the right to cancel.
- The Regulations create a statutory "cooling off period" to give the consumer time to cancel the contract, upon giving notice, if he so desires. This period is seven days if all the proper information has been supplied. It is extended by three months if the supplier fails to provide the appropriate information.
- Where a contract is cancelled, it is treated as though it had never existed. Suppliers are required to reimburse consumers within a maximum period of 30 days.

6. Prescribed terms and form and enforcement orders

The Act distinguishes between prescribed terms and prescribed form. The difference is important, in outline, because it is arguable that an agreement which is not in the prescribed form remains enforceable (or capable of being enforceable) whereas an agreement which fails to incorporate the prescribed terms is unenforceable.

Note also that if the agreement is cancellable and the prescribed notices have not been given then having the prescribed term in the agreement will not help the unenforceability pursuant to section 127(4).

Prescribed Forms
The prescribed forms are set out, for example, in the Consumer Credit (Agreement) Regulations 1983.

What are the Prescribed terms?

This begs the question as to what are the prescribed terms? They are contained in Schedule 6 of the 1983 Regulations. For DCS consumer credit agreements, the contract must contain the following (paragraphs 1 and 5 of Schedule 6):

> (a) a term stating the amount of credit; [paragraph 1] and a term stating how the debtor is to discharge his obligations under the agreement to make the repayments, which may be expressed by reference to a combination of any one of the following-
> (i) number of repayments;
> (ii) amount of repayments;
> (iii) frequency and timing of repayments;
> (iv) dates of repayment;
> (v) the manner in which any of the above may be determined; or in any other way, and any power of the creditor to vary what is payable.
>
> [Paragraph 5]

Arguably, also, it must include a term stating the rate of any interest on the credit to be provided under the agreement. Pursuant to paragraph 4 of Schedule 6, this prescribed term applies to the following fixed-sum credit agreements (for which see paragraph 9(a)–(c) of Schedule 1 of the 1983 Regulations):

> (a) agreements which do not specify either the intervals between repayments or the amounts of repayments or both the intervals and the amounts;
>
> (b) agreements under which the total amount payable by the debtor to discharge his indebtedness in respect of the amount of credit provided may vary according to any formula specified in the agreement having effect by reference to movements in the level of any index or to any other factor;
>
> (c) agreements which provide for a variation of, or permit the creditor to vary, (whether or not by reference to any index) the amount or rate of any item included in the total charge for credit after the relevant date.

In *Aggett* v *Aston Rothbury Factors Limited*, HHJ Overend, Exeter County Court, 6 July 2001, HHJ Overend stated:

> In my judgment, the thrust of paragraphs 9(b) and (c) relates to variations other than by way of simple additions of daily rates, and accordingly the agreement does not fall within the exceptions to paragraph 9 of Schedule 1. In those circumstances there is no need for the rate of interest to be referred to, even if it is zero percent, as neither agreement falls within the definition of paragraph 4 of Schedule 6.

The prescribed term for regulated consumer hire agreements is in paragraph 6 of Schedule 6 and consists of the following:

> A term stating how the hirer is to discharge his obligations under the agreement to pay the hire payments, which may be expressed by reference to a combination of any of the following– (a) number of payments; (b) amount of payments; (c) frequency and timing of payments; (d) dates of payments; (e) the manner in which any of the above may be determined; or in any other way, and any power of the owner to vary what is payable.

A term stating the amount of credit

Whether a particular agreement contains precisely the correct terms will depend upon its details. Perhaps the most controversial prescribed term is that requiring a statement of the amount of credit.

Whether a particular agreement contains precisely the correct terms will depend upon its details. It is perhaps unfortunate that the House of Lords did not give any guidance on this issue. Therefore, for the moment one must look to the comments of Scott V-C in the Court of Appeal.

In the Court of Appeal, the Claimant argued that it would not have been possible to have included the prescribed term. i.e., the amount of credit, since the length of the hire period would not be known. Scott V–C disagreed (at paragraph 71):

> But the daily rate of hire would be known and an estimate of the period of hire could be obtained from the garage that was repairing the damaged vehicle. In these circumstances paragraph 2(2) of the 1983 Regulations would, as I have read it, apply and would have allowed 1st Automotive to insert an estimate of the amount of credit with an indication of the assumptions on which the estimate was made. I do not accept that 1st Automotive could not have complied with the Regulations.

On its face, it would appear that he was wrong to suggest that this also applied to Schedule 6 since paragraph 2(2) of the 1983 Regulations allows estimates to be made only for those particulars set out in paragraphs 9 to 11 of Schedule 1 and not for those required by Schedule 6. Defendants may decide to argue this. However, Scott V–C's is the best judicial guidance there is on this point and it may be argued that he was filling a lacuna in the Act and Regulations. Further Claimants can point out the similarities between the relevant paragraphs in Schedule 1 and in Schedule 6.

Claimants may potentially argue that entering the price of the hire at the time was enough. If there is a three month clause, they can argue that that is the maximum period of hire and therefore the amount of credit can be worked out.

However, Defendants can argue that Scott V–C's comments do appear to suggest that in fact an estimate of the period of hire also needs to be included. Credit hire companies will therefore be able to argue that they have included the "amount of credit" if they have included the daily rate and the estimated time of hire. Even if such an estimate of the period of hire is included, Defendants will be able to argue that this is inadequate if the estimate does not actually end up being accurate as to the actual period of hire.

In the absence of any price being put on the contract at the time of the agreement, credit hire companies may potentially argue, depending on the facts, either that it was expressed orally or alternatively that the price was implied either as a reasonable price or indeed by a term in the contract which refers to the credit hire company's standard charges. Analogy may be drawn with the incorporation of terms on the back of train tickets.

However, whilst all of these methods may possibly be successful in arguing against an "uncertainty of terms" common law defence (see below), they are less likely to be successful in making up for the lack of a daily rate with regard to prescribed terms. Paragraph 1296 of Consumer Credit, edited by Professor Goode, states:

> Schedule 6 to the agreements regulations sets out the terms prescribed by s 61(1)(a) of the Act, that is, terms which are required to be contained in the executed agreement itself and not merely in some other document embodied in it by cross-reference.

Despite this weakness, however, the arguments may potentially still be there for Claimants to put if the particular facts of the case support them.

Cases on the amount of credit
In *Hatfield* v *Hiscock* [1998] CCLR 68; [1998] 6 CL 88, it was held to be enough that the price was on the agreement at the time it was made.

However, pursuant to *Dimond* in the Court of Appeal, Defendants have been able to argue that an estimate for the period of repairs is needed. Despite this, Claimants have had some success in arguing that simply entering the price was enough to satisfy the prescribed term requirement. Some cases are based on the fact that the damaged car was beyond economical repair and therefore an estimate of the repairs would not be appropriate. Others distinguish Scott V–C's comments on the basis that on the particular facts of the case, providing an estimate for the repairs would not be practicable. See *Stares* v *Deradour*, unreported, 24/5/1999, *Knight* v *Lawler*, unreported, Edmonton County Court, (DDJ Grant), 31/8/1999, *Marchant and Marchant* v *Brown*, unreported, 2/8/1999 (HHJ Poulton), *Knott* v *Stott*, unreported, 29/9/1999, *Jones* v *Lindon*, unreported, 26/7/1999.

In *Pitt-Miller* v *Patel*, HHJ Marr-Johnson, Mayor's & City County Court, 24 July 2001, the Judge stated:

> Even if, and I do not say they are, the other pleaded breaches [of the Act and/or Regulations] were made out, they could be remedied in enforcement proceedings against the Claimant and therefore the Defendant cannot seek to rely on those.

In *Wood* v *Gell*, HHJ Poulton, Canterbury County Court, 27 July 2001, it was argued for the Claimant that there was sufficient information to allow the debtor to calculate full liability and that the agreement was thus enforceable, relying upon *O'Hagan* v *Wright* (2001, CA (NI)) and further that the minor breaches would only render an agreement potentially unenforceable, and as such the Defendant could not rely upon such speculative matters.

The Judge mentioned that Scott V-C in *Dimond* considered enforceability and that he stated that an estimated total was required along with the assumptions upon which it was based. However, he went on:

> The Court of Appeal in Northern Ireland considered what Scott V-C had said and stated:
>
> "We would respectfully question the validity of such an expedient in relation to compliance with Schedule 6"
>
> (page 13 transcript)

LCJ Carswell then cites Regulation 2(2) Consumer Credit Agreements Order 1983 and comments that:

> we do not easily see how it could be invoked in respect of compliance with Schedule 6

He then refers to some judgments and goes on to say:

> One of the main objects of the 1974 Act is to ensure that there are no hidden charges and that the debtor knows where he stands. If he knows precisely how much per day the car hire charge will be, then he can calculate his liability exactly when he knows the length of the hiring, which will commonly by only when he gets his repaired car back on the road. The old

legal maxim *id cerum est quod redid potest* is both good sense and good law. We should accordingly be prepared to hold that the amount of credit has been sufficiently stated.

There is therefore, the VC's dictum and the Court of Appeal of Northern Ireland's decision. Neither are strictly binding upon me. I find the *O'Hagan* case more persuasive. The car hire charges in this case were very clearly stated and the liability could be easily calculated. This is a write off case and the total liability could be calculated as a matter of arithmetic.

In these circumstances the agreement is compliant with the Act and its Regulations. The attacks on the agreement thus fail and the Claimant is entitled to the claim for hire in full.

The difficulty with these cases is that if a requirement is not practicable, section 60(3) makes provision for an application for a waiver or variation of the requirement to be considered.

However, as Scott V-C made clear in the Court of Appeal in *Dimond*, this would not have retrospective effect in any event.

This difficulty stems from fitting credit hire into either fixed sum or running account credit even though it appears obvious to many people that credit was involved. This comes from the difficult-drafting of the Act. Scott V–C decided that credit was involved but then had to choose a category. Fixed-sum credit was the less tricky of the two but still faced the circular question of the indefinite (in other words not fixed) period of hire. He overcame this with reference to paragraph 2(2) of the 1983 Regulations. As mentioned above, although strictly this paragraph does not refer to Schedule 6 of the Regulations, it may be argued that perhaps he was filling a lacuna in the Act and Regulations.

The House of Lords did not explicitly tackle this problem but as mentioned Lord Hoffman's reference to paragraph 3 of the Exemption Order suggests that they were treating the agreement as a fixed-sum debtor-creditor-supplier agreement.

In *Aggett* v *Aston Rothbury Factors Limited*, HHJ Overend, Exeter County Court, 6 July 2001, HHJ Overend stated:

> For my part I have little hesitation in concluding that it cannot be said that the daily rates and surcharges inserted in either agreement can properly be described as "a term stating the amount of the credit" advanced... Further, there was no estimate of the total number of days that the hire period might have lasted, nor was there any references to the maximum financial amount which might result if the bailment ran to the full three month period.

On this basis the Judge held that the two agreements were irredeemably unenforceable by virtue of the provision of section 127(3) of the Act.

See also *Wilson* v *First County Trust* [2001] 3 WLR 42; [2001] 3 All ER 229; [2001] HRLR 7; [2001] Times 16 May; [2001] ILR 8 May and [2001] 2 WLR 302; [2000] Times 6 December on the amount of the credit.

A term stating how the debtor is to discharge his obligations under the agreement to make the repayments

The repayment terms will depend upon the particular provisions in each hire agreement. In *Aggett* v *Aston Rothbury Factors Limited*, HHJ Overend, Exeter County Court, 6 July 2001, HHJ Overend held that the agreement did make it clear, within the meaning of both paragraphs 5 and 6 of Schedule 6, how the debtor was to discharge his obligations.

Enforcement orders pursuant to section 65 and 127(1)

Even if the prescribed term were included in the agreement, there may be questions as to whether a court would enforce in the future in any event if the agreement is otherwise improperly executed.

It should be noted that in *Ketley* v *Gilbert* (above), with regard to the claimant's arguments in respect of sections 65(1) and 127(1) of the Act permitting enforcement, Brooke LJ stated:

> This point was not taken on the pleadings, and no evidence was adduced in relation to it before the district judge, who seems only to have been concerned with the preliminary point in relation to the enforceability of the hire agreement to which this judgment has been directed. Neither the district judge nor Judge Faulks referred to the point in their judgments. In these circumstances we told [the Claimant's counsel] that we could not entertain this point for the first time on the hearing of this appeal. If it is still open to the claimant to take the point in the court below (as to which we express no opinion, not having been shown the procedural direction, if any, which preceded the hearing before the district judge) then it should be properly formulated and any necessary evidence adduced before a judge is invited to decide the point.

Potentially, this suggests that the point would need to be pleaded and evidence would need to be given on the point.

Claimants may argue that they should recover the full amount on the basis that there is a potential liability.

Defendants may argue that the court should try and assess what is the possibility of enforcement in the future. On this basis, if the possibility is less than 50% then it may be argued that the Claimant has not proved his claim.

Alternatively, Defendants may argue that the court should only award a proportion of the hire charges based upon what percentage chance a Judge assesses the possibility of future enforcement. This could be on a similar assessment to those made in legal professional negligence cases. For a related approach see *Randall* v *Raper* (1858) El. Bl. & El. 84.

Further, for agreements made post-*Dimond*, the possibility of a credit hire company gaining the sympathy of the Court under section 65 may potentially become more remote and therefore the point may potentially become weaker.

There is little guidance on what principles would be applied with regard to an enforcement order. The notes to the Act provide some help but not with respect to the particular example of credit hire.

The starting point is section 127(1) of the Act which stipulates that the application shall be dismissed:

> "if, but (subject to subsections (8) and (4)) only if, it considers it just to do so having regard to- ... prejudice caused to any person by the contravention in question, and the degree of culpability for it...."

In *Hatfield* v *Hiscock* [1998] CCLR 68; [1998] 6 CL 88, *Stares* v *Deradour*, unreported, 24/5/1999, *Knight* v *Lawler*, unreported, Edmonton County Court, (DDJ Grant), 31/8/1999, *Marchant and Marchant* v *Brown*, unreported, 2/8/1999 (HHJ Poulton), *Knott* v *Stott*, unreported, 29/9/1999, *Jones* v *Lindon*, unreported, 26/7/1999, *Pitt-Miller* v *Patel*, HHJ Marr-Johnson, Mayor's & City County Court, 24 July 2001 and *Wood* v *Gell*, HHJ Poulton, Canterbury County Court, 27 July 2001 the court allowed the claim on the basis that an enforcement order may be made.

In *Aggett* v *Aston Rothbury Factors Limited*, HHJ Overend, Exeter County Court, 6 July 2001, HHJ Overend went on to examine the situation under section 65(1) obiter. It was argued on behalf of the Claimant that an incomplete consumer credit agreement was nevertheless an "existing liability", relying upon the decision of the Court of Appeal in *R* v *Modupe* [1999] Goode Consumer Credit Reports 1595. The Judge stated:

> It seems to me that the decision in *R* v *Modupe* was concerned with a wholly different legal proposition, namely whether an incomplete consumer

credit agreement was an existing agreement for the purposes of the Theft Act 1974. It was not concerned with the question whether hire charges arising from an incomplete credit hire agreement would be recoverable from a tort feasor, even though they had not yet been paid to the credit hire company.

Applying general principles, the court needs to assess the prospect of the hire charges being recovered from the driver, despite non-compliance with the statutory provisions of the Consumer Credit Act and despite the failure of the credit hire company to obtain the necessary credit or hire brokerage licenses.

Section 65 makes it clear that a court order is required before an improperly executed agreement can be enforced. In the light of the court's findings and reasoning relating to the deficiencies in specifying the "amount of credit" required under para 1 of Schedule 6, it seems to follow that there would also be a breach of the similar provisions relating to "amount of credit" (paras 6 and 7) contained in Schedule 1 and in relation to the precise specification of "hire payments" and "other payments" in Schedule 3. These deficiencies would characterise the agreement as improperly executed (section 61), bringing into play the requirement to obtain an order under section 65.

On such an application, section 127(1) stipulates that the application shall be dismissed:

"if....only if it considers it just to do so having regard to:

(i) prejudice caused to any person by the contravention in question, and the degree of culpability for it...."

I agree with Mr Hammill that the prospect of a court granting the s.65 order would not be high where – as here – the evidence was that the claimant would not have entered into the transaction if he had appreciated that he might have had to pay the full amount of the hire charges in the sums finally claimed by Crash Care, and that he was committing himself to them by signing the hire agreements. Had there been compliance with the provisions of the Statute, then it is likely that this Claimant would not have entered into the agreements. In those circumstances, I find that the chances of a court making a section 65 order low.

That leaves the question of assessing the prospect of the Director making an order under section 40. It was conceded during the trial that no application to the Director had been made for a section 40(2) order by Crash Care or by their factors. No evidence was given about the prospects of such an order being granted, should the application be made in the future.

It seems to me that on the state of the evidence before the Court the prospects of Crash Care being able to recover the credit hire charges from the claimant are negligible...

...For those additional reasons, I find for the Defendant in relation to the sole issue before the Court, namely the recoverability of the hire charges.

7. Human Rights Law

The effect of the Consumer Credit Act 1974 was that contracts become automatically unenforceable for relatively minor technical breaches. It has been argued on behalf of the creditors that this infringes their human rights.

The human rights arguments were argued before the House of Lords in *Wilson* v *Secretary of State for Trade and Industry* [2003] UKHL 40. Mrs Wilson had pawned her BMW convertible for six months in return for £5,000. She did not repay the loan. Instead she commenced proceedings in the Kingston-upon-Thames County Court arguing that the agreement was unenforceable as it did not comply with the prescribed terms. From modest beginnings, the case snowballed. There were interventions from the Attorney General on behalf of the Secretary of State for Trade and Industry, the Speaker of the House of Commons, four motor insurers and the Finance and Leasing Association.

The Court of Appeal held that the agreement was unenforceable. Mrs Wilson was able to keep the loan without paying interest and to recover her car. However Morritt V-C was concerned about this result: he thought it might violate article 6(1) of the European Convention on Human Rights and article 1 of the First Protocol. The hearing was adjourned to allow submissions on that point. The Court of Appeal made a declaration of incompatibility. The Secretary of State appealed to the House of Lords.

In a decision of some important to human rights lawyers, the House of Lords held that the Human Rights Act 1998 did not apply to Mrs Wilson's contract. The reason was that her cause of action accrued before section 3(1) of the Human Rights Act 1998 came into force. This meant that the House of Lords did not need to go on to address the remaining human rights arguments. Their opinions on this point are strictly obiter.

Article 6(1)
Article 6(1) guarantees everyone the right to a fair expeditious and public trial of disputes about their civil rights. It includes the implied right of access to the courts. It is not a means of creating new civil rights: it only means that existing civil rights have to be capable of being submitted to a Judge for adjudication (*c.f. Fayed* v *UK* (1994) 18 EHRR 393).

Lord Nicholls held at paragraph 35 that "the crucial question…is whether, as a matter of substance, the relevant provision of national law has the effect of preventing an issue which ought to be decided by a court from being so decided".

He analysed the creditor's complaint as being that: "section 127(3) of the Consumer Credit Act has the effect that a regulated agreement is not enforceable unless a document containing all the prescribed terms is signed by the debtor". In his view this did not engage article 6(1). The reason is that it is:

> a restriction on the rights that a creditor acquires under a regulated agreement. It does not bar access to a court to decide whether the case is caught by the restriction. It does bar a court from exercising any discretion over whether to make an enforcement order. But in taking that power away from the court the legislature was not encroaching on territory which ought properly to be the province of the courts in a democratic society.
>
> (paragraph 36)

The other four members of the House of Lords agreed that article 6(1) was simply not engaged by this case.

Article 1 of the First Protocol
The issues raised by article 1 of the First Protocol provoked more debate in the House of Lords. It provides:

> every natural and legal person is entitled to the peaceful enjoyment of his possessions. No-one shall be deprived of his possessions except in the public interest and subject to the conditions provided for by law…the preceding provisions shall not, however, in any way impair the right of a State to enforce such laws as it deems necessary to control the use of property in accordance with the general interest.

The majority of the House of Lords rejected the creditors arguments for two reasons. First they thought that article 1 of the First Protocol was not engaged. Second they thought if it was engaged, the Consumer Credit Act was proportionate and reasonable.

In relation to whether article 1 was engaged, Lord Hope held at paragraph 109 that article 1 of the First Protocol was not engaged. His reason was that the lender never had an absolute or unqualified right to enforce the agreement or property rights. Article 1 could not be used to confer absolute rights, where they did not previously exist.

Lord Scott at paragraph 168 thought that article 1 "is directed to interference with existing possessions or property rights." Section 127(3) prevented the lender from ever having the right to enforce the agreement. Accordingly article 1 was not engaged.

Lord Nicholls on the other hand thought that article 1 of the First Protocol was engaged. He considered that the effect of the relevant provisions in the Consumer Credit Act was a statutory deprivation of the lender's rights of property rather than a mere delimitation of the extent of those rights. Quite simply "the lender's right were extinguished in favour of the borrower by legislation for which the state is responsible".

On the second point however all their Lordship agreed: the provisions in the Consumer Credit Act did not violate article 1 Protocol 1.

Lord Nicholls stated at paragraph 68 that inherent in article 1 is the need to hold a fair balance between the public interest and the fundamental rights of creditors. It was common ground that article 1 pursued a legitimate aim: protecting vulnerable persons from exploitation. Therefore the point turned on whether the means employed were proportionate to the legitimate aim.

At paragraphs 74 – 78 Lord Nicholls concluded that the means employed were proportionate. He thought that it was open to Parliament to make compliance with formalities a prerequisite to the enforceability of certain contracts. A uniform solution applied across the board may be the most appropriate was to deal with the problem: a tailor made solution considering the facts of each case may fail to protect the vulnerable. Accordingly he held that section 127(3) was compatible with article 1 of the First Protocol.

Lord Hobhouse agreed that the Consumer Credit Act did not go beyond the measures which are justifiable under that article. Lord Hope expressed agreement with Lord Nicholls on this point.

Lord Scott similarly held at paragraph 169 that the provision in the Consumer Credit Act could not be characterised as disproportionate. The reason is that all legal systems have attempted to control money lending transactions. The control measures reflect the vulnerability of those members of the public who need to borrow.

Although, as set out above, these opinions were obiter, they carry great weight. Full argument was held on the issues and the judgements are detailed. The result is that it appears fruitless for creditors to argue human rights points in credit hire cases.

The position has of course been altered with the advent of the Consumer Credit Act 2006. From 6 April 2007, the provisions regarding automatic unenforceability have been repealed. This means that there is likely to be even less scope for human rights based arguments. For further details see Chapter 5.

8. Consent: section 173(3)

Section 173(3) provides:

> Notwithstanding subsection (1), a provision of this Act under which a thing may be done in relation to any person on an order of the court or the Director only shall not be taken to prevent its being done at any time with that person's consent given at that time, but the refusal of such consent shall not give rise to any liability.

Subject to the facts of the particular case, the Claimant may decide to argue that he consents to breaches of the Act and therefore to the enforceability of the contract. The Defendant may argue either that this is prevented by other provisions of the Act or that such a consent would be a failure to mitigate. The Claimant in *Dimond* elected not to run this argument at all.

9. 'Spot' hire agreements

In *Dimond*, one of the terms in the written agreement expressly provided for payment to be deferred. This made it easy for the House of Lords to decide that credit was provided.

Not all "credit hire" agreements are so transparent. Where an agreement does not include a term deferring payment, it may be more difficult for Defendants to argue that any credit is provided at all. The fact that an agreement has not been enforced might potentially be a gratuitous indulgence or a forbearance on the part of the credit hire company. It is arguable that this would not amount to a contractual deferment of debt.

The Claimants arguments were accepted in the case of *Wilkins and Goodfellow* v *Gowrings Food Services*, unreported, DJ Tromans, 12/8/1999. In particular, the District Judge relied upon paragraph 442 of Professor Goode's *Encyclopedia of Consumer Credit*.

It should perhaps be noted that the case of Wilkins went even further and found that there was no provision of credit where the agreement catered both for the possibility of payment on demand and the lessor allowing the hirer credit at his discretion. Four particular points were made.

First, the agreement was different from that in *Dimond* since it did not provide an actual time for payment but instead stated that it may be on demand. Therefore, it was held, according to Scott V–C's definition, there was no credit since there was not an initial time for payment. Whilst this may miss the point that Scott V–C appeared to be talking about a putative time for payment in the absence of express provision, it remains an argument.

Second, the provision of credit remained at the lessor's discretion on the face of the agreement. It provided that where the vehicle was let to the hirer as a result of the hirer's own vehicle being un-roadworthy as a result of a road traffic accident, the company may (but shall not be obliged to) grant the hirer credit on rentals. The Judge found that the provision of credit would have amounted to a variation of the agreement and there had been no evidence of any such variation.

Third, there was no credit since Professor Goode's definition of credit in paragraph 443 of the *Encyclopedia* defined it as an option given to the debtor and not, as in the present case, an option retained by the debtor.

Fourth, there was evidence of an invoice addressed to the Second Claimant and apparently sent to his Solicitors which was dated one day after the hire ended. Therefore, the Judge held, the company had made a demand for payment and the Second Claimant was under a contractual requirement to comply with that demand.

On the other hand, in *Davis* v *Izatt*, unreported, 1/9/1999, DJ Polden held that an apparent spot hire agreement did provide credit. When taken with the circumstances as a whole it was clear that the Claimant was told that he would not have to pay. No demand was made either on supply or return of the vehicle. The Claimant said that the charges would not be paid until the conclusion of this case and therefore, there had been a deferral of payment. The agreement fell within the definition in *Dimond*. See also *Katon* v *O'Reilly*, unreported, 13/9/99.

Only time will tell how these points will be received in other cases.

10. Act only applies to individuals

It should be noted that both section 8 and section 15 of the Act clearly state that they apply where the debtor or hirer is an "individual". Section 189 of the Act states that "individual" "includes a partnership or other unincorporated body of persons not consisting entirely of bodies corporate".

The Act does not therefore protect any form of corporate entity and so a Consumer Credit Act defence (though not necessarily the other arguments) would fail against such a body.

Another argument in this regard is that since the title of the Act only refers to "Consumer", the Act should only apply to consumers, either as defined under European law or perhaps pursuant to the Unfair Contract Terms Act 1977. Therefore, for example, a mini-cab driver who is self employed and who hires a cab after an accident would not be covered by the Act even though he would come within the definition of individual. It may be added that the *contra preferentum* rule would not apply in this case.

This argument is unlikely to carry much success but authority is still awaited.

Chapter 7

RESIDUAL LIABILITY FOR HIRE: COMMON LAW ARGUMENTS

There are numerous common law arguments which may surround the enforceability of credit hire agreements. It should be noted that some of these common law arguments may also be utilised to attack or support clauses in contracts which purport to exempt the agreement from the Act.

However before descending into the detail of these issues, there is an overarching problem for Defendants which is common to all these arguments. This is the "does it matter anyway" question (*c.f.* Chapter 4). The point is that in *Dimond* v *Lovell* the agreements were automatically unenforceable by virtue of the strict provisions of the Consumer Credit Act 1974. There is no such automatic unenforceability provision for these common law arguments.

Thus it is open to Claimants to argue that it does not matter if the Defendant can establish that there might be an estoppel (for example) as between Claimant and hire company. Until a court holds that there is an estoppel between Claimant and hire company, the Claimant remains potentially liable for the hire charges and hence the Defendant does too. The Claimant is not obliged to enter uncertain litigation against the hire company in order to mitigate his loss. Thus it is arguable that any of these common law arguments represent a futile and expensive attempt to look behind the terms of an apparently valid contract.

The counter argument for Defendants is that a contract is either enforceable or unenforceable. It cannot be half enforceable. The court can be invited to determine at the hearing whether the contract is enforceable or not. The downside of this is that it might well require the hire company to be joined into proceedings.

Oral assurances

One of the most common issues regards oral assurances before the making of the contract. These may include assurances made by the hire company to the effect that the Claimant will not have to pay or that no payment will be due until after the claim has come to an end with the Third Party (which may be longer than the prescribed twelve months).

Credit hire companies may argue that any such assurances were not made by any of their servants or agents. Further, even if they were, the Claimant would be bound by what he had signed, in other words relying on the supposed 'parol evidence rule'.

They may also rely upon the five guidelines to the interpretation of contracts set out by Lord Hoffmann in *ICS* v *West Bromwich BS* (above) to suggest that oral evidence should only be adduced when there is an ambiguity in the written contract.

However, there have been a number of modern cases which have whittled away at the parol evidence rule to the extent that it may plausibly be argued that it is meaningless today. Different cases have produced different analyses and conclusions. Oral assurances may support the arguments set out below.

The fact that an agreement has not been enforced after twelve months may possibly add weight to some of the arguments in the context of exemption clauses.

A helpful case for Defendants in respect of the common law arguments is that of *Carmichael and Leese* v *National Power PLC* [1999] 1 W.L.R. 2042 in which the House of Lords held that the construction of documents as a question of law did not apply when the intention of parties, objectively ascertained, had to be gathered partly from documents but also from oral exchanges and conduct. It was then a question of fact. This may help with the use of any oral assurances or representations by or on behalf of the hire company.

Partly oral, partly in writing
The oral assurance may give rise to a contract which is partly oral and partly in writing. The assurance may be binding preventing the hire company from relying on provisions which contradict it. See Roskill LJ in *J. Evans & Son (Portsmouth) Limited* v *Andrea Merzario Limited* [1976] 1 WLR 1078.

Collateral contracts

Depending on the facts, it may also be argued that the main credit hire agreement was entered into by the Claimant only in consideration of a promise by the credit hire company that they would never enforce the agreement against him. In such a case, it could be argued that a collateral contract has arisen. Therefore, the Claimant cannot rely on a term in the main contract suggesting that he has a liability if it is contradicted by a term in the collateral contract suggesting that in reality he does not. Such a proposition is supported by the case of *City and Westminster Properties (1934) Ltd* v *Mudd* [1959] 1 Ch 129 and Lord Denning MR in *J. Evans & Son (Portsmouth) Limited* v *Andrea Merzario Limited* (above).

Against this, Claimants and credit hire companies may argue that there was never any legal intention to enter into a collateral contract. Further, credit hire companies may claim that any such suggestion was mere sales talk and did not amount to a legal representation. Finally, it should be noted that in at least one of the cases in *Giles* v *Thompson*, the publicity had suggested that the car would be free. However at [1993] 3 All ER 321, 364H–365B, Lord Mustill did suggest that this practice should be changed.

Estoppel

The oral assurance may create an estoppel preventing the hire company from relying on provisions which contradict it. See *City and Westminster Properties (1934) Ltd.* Estoppel is usually thought of as a shield rather than a sword: the Claimant could use estoppel to defend a claim brought by the hire company but could not base a claim on it. This limits the usefulness of estoppel to Defendant insurers.

Repugnance

Any clause contradicting the oral assurance may risk not being enforced as being "repugnant" to the assurance. See Lord Denning MR in *Mendelssohn* v *Normand* [1970] 1 QB 177 at 184.

Misrepresentation

The oral assurance may amount to a misrepresentation making the contract voidable. See *L'Estrange* v *Graucob* [1934] 2 KB 394, *Couchman* v *Hill* [1947] 1 KB 554, *Thomas Witter Limited* v *TBP Industries Limited* [1996] 2 All ER 573, *Bleakley* v *Grimway* [1998] 2 CL 125, *Rendle* v *Hicks* [1998] 2 CL 126 and *Pinder* v *Martin* [1998] 11 CL 160. See also the case of *County NatWest Bank Ltd* v *Barton and Others* [1999] Times, 29 July (on fraudulent misrepresentation) and the case of *EA Grimstead & Son Limited* v *McGarrigan*, Court of Appeal, [1999] Lawtel 27 October (in the context of entire agreement clauses).

This will be harder to prove since a positive misrepresentation will be needed and also proof that this induced the Claimant to enter into the contract.

In any event, Claimants may argue that since the agreement is simply voidable and not void, it remains enforceable by a court. A liability therefore remains for which it can be argued the Claimant should be compensated by the Defendant. Defendants may say that in any event, a failure to rescind the contract would be a failure to mitigate.

Further, they may argue that a Claimant does not have to take the risk of uncertain litigation against a third party (see *McGregor on Damages* at paragraph 327, citing the dictum of Harman J in *Pilkington* v *Wood* [1953] Ch. 770 that, "the so-called duty to mitigate does not go so far as to oblige the injured party, even under an indemnity, to embark on a complicated and difficult piece of litigation against a third party". So, too, it may be argued, a Claimant does not have to take the risk of being sued by a third party.

Credit hire companies may claim that any such representation was in any event mere sales talk and did not amount to a legal representation. Further, that it was not that which induced the Claimant to enter into the contract. Finally, as with collateral contracts (above), they may point to the case of Giles v Thompson and the fact that the contracts still survived.

"Entire agreement" clauses

A case which may potentially help Claimants is that of *EA Grimstead & Son Ltd* v *McGarrigan*, CA [1999] Lawtel 27 October. The Court of Appeal analysed, it seems obiter, the effect of an entire agreement clause coupled with an overlapping clause acknowledging that the purchaser had not relied on any warranty etc. other than those contained in the agreement. They held that it was not open to a purchaser to assert that he did not rely on a representation which was made to him and afterwards say that that was nothing more than what he thought was the position at the time. He must be taken to know, at the time when he entered in to the agreement, what representation he was relying upon.

Further, an acknowledgement of non-reliance, in the form which appeared in the two clause, was capable of operating as an evidential estoppel. It was apt to prevent the party who had given the acknowledgement from asserting in subsequent litigation against the party to whom it had been given that it was not true. That was a proper use of an acknowledgement of that nature which had become a common feature of professionally drawn commercial contracts.

However, Defendants may point to what the Court also said. The Defendant had not relied on estoppel in his Defence. Whilst the acknowledgements of non-reliance contained in the two clauses were clear and unequivocal, in the absence of such pleading it was not safe to assume that the Judge would have reached the conclusion that the Defendant entered into the agreement on the basis that the purchaser was not relying on the representations made. For those reasons, which differed from those given by the Judge, the Court would not have been prepared to hold that the Defendant could rely on the acknowledgements of non-reliance in the agreement.

The Court also held that in respect of the argument based on the Misrepresentation Act 1967, it was wholly fair and reasonable that the purchaser should seek his remedies (if any) within the four corners of the agreement; and should not be permitted to rely on pre-contractual representations which were, deliberately, not reflected in contractual warranties.

This suggests that Claimants would have to plead any such argument. In any event, much will depend upon the particular facts.

Further, Defendants may argue, depending upon the facts, that the clause is unfair pursuant to the Unfair Terms Regulations or alternatively rely upon arguments based upon cases such as *Interfoto* mentioned above. Other common law arguments may also apply.

The case of *McGarrigan* was applied in *Fleet Mobile Tyres Ltd* v *Stone and Anor* [2006] EWHC 1947 and quoted with approval in *Six Continents Hotels Inc* v *Event Hotels GMBH* [2006] EWHC 2317. In the context of entire agreement clauses, the following cases should also be noted: *McGrath* v *Shah* [1989] 57 P & CR 452; *Deepak Fertilisers and Petrochemicals Corporation* v *ICI Chemicals* [1998] 2 Lloyds Rep 139; CA [1999] 1 Lloyds Rep 387

Certainty of terms

Defendants may also be able to argue that a credit hire agreement was so vague and/or uncertain that it did not give rise to a binding contract. For example, the Claimant may not have been aware either of the rates of hire or the hire company's standard terms and conditions at the time that he signed the agreement (see *Chitty on Contracts*, 27th Edition, paragraphs 2–099 to 2–104 and for an example, *Scammell & Nephew* v *Ouston* [1941] AC 251. In *Conway* v *Lagou* [2000] 2 CL, HHJ Cowell found an agreement to be void for uncertainty of terms).

Against this, Claimants will be able to argue that terms are either implied or were oral or were incorporated by a term in the contract (as with train tickets). Further, they can argue the parol evidence rule: that the Claimant is bound by what he has signed in the absence of express evidence to the contrary.

In *Prescott* v *Hamnett* [1998] 11 CL 158 and *Pinder* v *Martin* [1998] 11 CL 160 hire agreements were signed where the price was not on the agreement at the time. The claims for hire failed in both cases. The first on the basis simply that the Claimant did not have a responsibility to pay, the second on the basis that there was no contract and therefore no loss.

One case has even held that not putting the price on the document was a representation that the hire was free and any suggestion to the contrary would make it a misrepresentation. Therefore hire charges were not recoverable on that ground.

Agreement not signed at time of taking possession of car

What is the position if the Claimant does not sign the credit hire agreement at the time that they accept delivery of the replacement vehicle?

In *Carson* v *Tazaki Foods Ltd* (25 August 2005), the Claimant spoke with the hire company on the telephone. She then received a hire car for three days. The hire documents were sent to her in the post but she did not actually sign the papers until months later. It was held that the Claimant entered into a contract with the hire company orally by telephone and that the terms of that contract were identical to the subsequent written terms. The best evidence of the terms of agreement were the signed written documents, even where that signature was late.

The Claimant sought to take the point further and argued that the contract ought not to be placed under close scrutiny because it was not relevant to the question whether the Claimant acted reasonably. The court however accepted that close analysis of contract was a feature of credit hire litigation. It is a vital part of the Claimant proving his loss. However the Judge went on to comment that the evidential burden on the Claimant would be light in such cases and it would be very difficult for Defendants to succeed on such points.

A similar result was reached in *Borley* v *Reed* 20 October 2005. The Judge found that during the preliminary telephone call, the Claimant agreed to use the hire company subject to the detailed terms and conditions which would be sent through to her. This arrangement is commonplace. The content of the telephone call did not constitute a concluded oral agreement. The Judge went on to criticise the disproportionate approach taken by the Defendant insurer. He said "I do not understand why the law should contemplate with equanimity the determined attempt on the part of the tortfeasor's insurers to meddle in that sensible and beneficial arrangement".

Variation: section 82

Where it is clear that a regulated agreement has been varied since it was made, two points need to be made. First, if the agreement was unenforceable in the first place, then the Claimant will have suffered no loss and if a Claimant later signs an agreement to try and make it enforceable this is likely to be construed as a failure to mitigate.

Second, any variation of a regulated agreement if it is done under a power contained in the original agreement would not take effect until notice of it has been given to the debtor or hirer in the prescribed manner (see section 82(1)). The other provisions of section 82 may also need to be taken into account when an agreement has been varied in some way.

If the agreement was signed after the Claimant took possession of the car it may be argued that the terms and conditions to which the Claimant signed up were not part of the original agreement. Defendants will concentrate on the issue of the original agreement. This may therefore mean that an exemption clause or a ninety days clause has no effect. Alternatively, that the residual liability clause has no effect and if the Claimant was under the impression that the car was free and he signed up to nothing to the contrary at the time then the agreement would be unenforceable as champertous.

Claimants may try and argue that the written contract was simply confirmation of what was originally agreed or alternatively that it was a valid variation of the original agreement. In this regard, they need to be aware of section 82.3 of the Act which provides:

> if the earlier agreement is a regulated agreement but (apart from this sub section) the modifying agreement is not then… It shall be treated as a regulated agreement.

Signing after the car is taken out may also affect a twelve month/4 payment exemption clause since time for the exemption order may start running at the time the car was taken out but time for the agreement may start running at the time the agreement was signed.

In *Clark* v *Ardington Electrical Services and others*, HHJ Harris, Oxford County Court, 14 September 2001, HHJ Harris stated:

> A further point was made that in the case of Dr Sen [one of the Claimants] there was a modification of his original agreement. The argument was that he first entered into an oral agreement which would have been regulated, and then subsequently into a written modifying agreement in terms drafted to achieve exemption. This would not be effective by virtue of section 82.3 ... I think that Mr Flaux [Counsel for the Defendant] made this submission with a little less than his normal high level of conviction and I accept Mr Milligan's [Counsel for the Claimant] submission that it is not sound. There was no sufficient concluded contract before the signed agreement. What was done before then was undertaken in expectation of the signed agreement.
>
> Accordingly I find that these arguments were exempt agreements and are not to be set aside for failing to achieve exemption."

Where there is no signed agreement at all, the Claimant's case will probably be at its weakest. In *Allen* v *Drake* [1999] 5 CL 49 it was held that the claim was a hopeless one and that the absence of a signed agreement was so fundamental that it must have been obvious to the Claimant's solicitors that the court was not going to allow the hire charges. Nor were hire charges recovered in *Fletcher* v *Sutton* [1998] 1 CL 153, *Brumant* v *Boyle* [1999] CL in which there was no signed contractual documentation by the Claimant.

A different but related case should also be noted. In *Hitchens* v *General Guarantee Corporation Limited* [2001] Times 13 March, the Court of Appeal held that there was sufficient evidence in the instant case to show that the finance company had entered into a hire purchase agreement with the purchaser of a car, notwithstanding that the finance company had not signed the written agreement, because it had orally accepted the offer to enter into the agreement on the day of the purchase.

The appeal was by General Guarantee Corp Ltd ("GGC") from the decision of Christopher Purchas QC sitting as a deputy judge of the High Court. The appeal raised a question as to the application of section 27 of the Hire Purchase Act 1964. GGC argued that the Judge erred in holding that section 27 of the Act applied to the instant case. The ground of appeal was from the finding that the agreement was entered into on the 22 February 1995, when R took possession of the vehicle, as opposed to the 28 February 1995 when GGC put its signature to the agreement. In the interim period, R had sold the car to W, who had in turn sold it to the claimant. GGC argued that the dealer had made a preliminary bailment when he delivered the vehicle to R, and not a bailment under the agreement as the Judge had found. Accordingly, GGC argued that s.27 of the 1964 Act did not apply.

It was held, dismissing the appeal that the difficulty for GGC was that the Judge had found that GGC had orally accepted the agreement by telephone on 22 February 1995. Ordinary contractual principles applied in cases where the express terms of a hire purchase agreement did not preclude acceptance on behalf of the finance company made orally or by conduct (*Carlyle Finance Ltd* v *(1) Pallas Industrial Finance Ltd (2) John Burgess* [1999] RTR 281). Whilst GGC accepted that principle, it sought to show that the instant case was distinguishable from Carlyle (above). However, the Judge was entitled to infer from the evidence before him, that on the balance of probabilities, there was oral acceptance by GGC of an offer by R to enter into the agreement on 22 February 1995. The Judge was accordingly entitled to hold that, on contractual principles (Carlyle (above)), there was a binding agreement entered into on 22 February 1995, and ownership of the vehicle passed on that date. Such a finding was in line with commercial efficacy as it was unlikely that a dealer would release a vehicle to a purchaser without being able to rely on the finance company satisfying the purchase price. The requirements of section 27 of the 1964 Act were satisfied.

Non est factum

Defendants may also consider pleading the doctrine of *non est factum*. This doctrine applies where (see *The Law of Contract* by Sir J.C. Smith, 2nd Edition, pages 18–19 and for an example, *Gallie* v *Lee* [1971] AC 1004): A's signature has been procured by the fraud of B; B's fraud was such as to lead A to believe that the contents of the document were fundamentally different from the facts; and A was not guilty of negligence in so signing.

However, Claimants will be quick to point out that fraud needs to be pleaded here and that this is a very serious allegation to make. Defendants must therefore take care in so arguing but credit hire companies must obviously avoid any of their employees so behaving.

Recoverable charges limited to terms of contract

It may sometimes be the case that hire agreements limit the period of hire to a certain number of days but the actual period of hire exceeds this. Credit hire companies can argue that by hiring for a longer period, the lessor has effectively waived that term. Furthermore, that whilst the written contract may not cover the extra period there would be an implied contract at the same price for the extended period. Alternatively, keeping the car constitutes an affirmation of a new contract on the same terms as the original one. From a different perspective, the Claimant may argue that he has retained the car in breach of the original agreement and for which he would be liable to the credit hire company for damages.

However, Defendants can argue that this would not constitute a genuine waiver and that the only charges recoverable should be for that limited number of days. *Sullivan* v *Paul* [1998] 6 CL 91 and *Foskett* v *Brown* [1998] 6 CL 90 were such cases in which the Defendant's arguments were successful. Defendants may also argue that a breach of contract by the Defendant would constitute a failure to mitigate on his part.

Details of hire car and damaged car

If insurers discover that a credit hire company is in fact hiring the vehicle from another company, they may argue that the charges are excessive if they are more than that other company are charging. However, post-*Dimond*, such a submission may carry less weight.

Privilege and proportionality may also come into play.

Insurers may also investigate whether the credit hire company is in breach of any clauses forbidding them from sub-letting the car. If so, arguments regarding inducing a breach of contract or public policy arguments as to unenforceability may be raised.

Insurers may also check whether in fact the Claimant owned the car he was driving at the time of the accident and whether he was properly insured for the use to which he was putting it at that point.

In particular if the Claimant was not insured to drive his own car additional arguments are open to the Defendant. First it can be argued that provision of an insured and legally driveable hire car represents betterment since the damaged vehicle was not insured. Similar arguments apply if it was unlawful for the Claimant to drive his car because he had not paid road tax or the vehicle had failed its MOT. It could also apply to persons disqualified from driving or taxi drivers carrying on business without the appropriate licence.

Second it can be argued that the whole claim for hire charges is founded on the illegal act of driving without insurance. In *Hewison* v *Meridien Shipping* [2002] EWCA Civ 1821 the Claimant was seeking damages for personal injury. His claim included loss of earnings. He was employed as a crane operator. He was epileptic. He had not disclosed this to his employer: such disclosure would have prevented him working in this capacity.

The Court of Appeal asked the question "is the relevant part of the claim based substantially on an illegal act?"

The majority went on to hold that to recover for loss of earnings the Claimant would have to show that he would have continued in his job but for the accident. In order to keep working in that capacity he would have had to continue to deceive his employer. In so doing he would commit the criminal offence of obtaining a pecuniary advantage by deception. Accordingly his claim for loss of earnings was dismissed.

However it is also well known that Claimants can recover loss of earnings even where they did not pay tax or national insurance on their pre-accident earnings *c.f. Newman* v *Fowkes* [2002] EWCA Civ 519.

On which side of the line does a claim for car hire in these circumstances fall? It is certainly arguable that the claim rests on the assertion that but for the accident the Claimant would have continued driving his own vehicle. If he had done so he would be acting illegally. This is arguably more than merely collateral.

However Claimants may argue that they could have insured the vehicle at any time. It was open to them to bring the illegality to an end at any time and to continue driving legally. Whether this submission is credible will depend on the facts of the case. It is certainly arguable that this reduces the significance of the illegality.

Chapter 8

RATES

The final area of dispute which arose in *Dimond* v *Lovell* regarded how to measure the Claimant's loss. This reflected a larger dispute between the insurance and credit hire industries. Insurers have long complained that credit hire rates are usually more than equivalent "spot" or non-credit hire rates. This has usually been justified by the credit hire companies on the basis that they are providing a different service from spot hire companies. In its clearest form, the dispute might centre on evidence given by an insurance company as to equivalent spot hire rates and evidence from a representative of a credit hire company as to equivalent credit hire rates. Each might argue that in order to determine the reasonableness of the rates, their figures should be the ones used to compare with those in dispute.

Although the speeches on this issue were strictly obiter full argument was heard on it. They therefore carry considerable weight. It would be a bold Judge in the County Courts who would depart from them.

Before analysing the speeches of the House of Lords it is worth looking first at how the Court of Appeal tackled the issue.

The Court of Appeal

By a majority of two to one, the Court of Appeal held in effect that the correct comparison in determining reasonableness was with other credit hire rates. However, Scott V–C's comments did leave the door open for the case to be distinguished, particularly when read in conjunction with the different view of Judge LJ on this issue.

Given that this is not the clearest part of the judgments, we will set out these parts of the judgments in some detail. First, Scott V–C at paragraphs 93–95:

> The standard of conduct required of a plaintiff in order to avoid charges of a failure to mitigate his damage is not a particularly onerous one. As it is put in *McGregor on Damages*, 16th Ed., in para. 322:–

"Although the plaintiff must act with the defendant's as well as with his own interests in mind, he is only required to act reasonably and the standard of reasonableness is not high in view of the fact that the defendant is an admitted wrongdoer."

In the present case it is clear from the evidence that Mrs Dimond, or perhaps her husband, simply accepted their insurance broker's recommendation to use the services on offer from 1st Automotive. It was, in my opinion, eminently reasonable for them to have done so. A broker is more likely to have a knowledge of the services on offer that an individual could acquire even after a tedious hour or so with Yellow Pages and a telephone. It cannot be the law that a plaintiff who asks for the advice of a broker and does not herself telephone around to test the market is failing to take reasonable steps to mitigate her damage. The broker was, of course, her agent. Should he have tested the car hire market in order to advise her whom she should approach for a replacement vehicle? There was no evidence from the broker, so what, if any, thought he gave to ordinary car hire firms one cannot tell. But it seems to me that he was entitled to take the view that a firm like 1st Automotive, which would provide Mrs Dimond with a suitable vehicle and relieve her from the worry of having to argue with Mr Lovell's insurers about recovery and from the worry of any necessary litigation, would provide a service that she could reasonably decide to take. Mr McLaren [for the Defendant] pointed out, correctly, that damages for worry and for the nuisance caused by having to deal with the consequences of an accident are not recoverable. It does not follow, however, that an injured party's decision to hire a replacement vehicle from a company which, as well as supplying the vehicle, will relieve her of the worry and nuisance which would normally result from the accident is a decision which fails to take sufficient account of the Defendants interest. Nor, in my view, does the fact that the company's hire charges are higher than those of ordinary car hire companies necessarily lead to a different conclusion. The evidence in the case was that 1st Automotive's charges were in line with those of other companies offering a similar service.

It is, after all, a question of fact whether a plaintiff has acted unreasonably in incurring the item of expense that is sought to be recovered as damages. The recorder held that Mrs Dimond had acted reasonably in hiring her replacement vehicle from 1st Automotive. In so holding he was implicitly also holding that in doing so Mrs Dimond had not failed to take account of the interests of Mr Lovell. The evidence before him entitled him, in my judgment, to come to that conclusion. I do not think it was obligatory for Mrs Dimond to shop around or to go to an ordinary car hire company. It was reasonable to choose the special niche service on offer from 1st Automotive. If the agreement Mrs Dimond entered into with 1st Automotive had been enforceable against her, I would, in agreement with the Recorder, have held her to be entitled to recover as damages the charges payable under it.

Thorpe LJ simply followed the judgment of Scott V–C with "I agree". This was followed by Judge LJ at paragraphs 98–103:

> With the exception of the last question, described in argument as "mitigation" of the plaintiff's damage, I agree with the reasoning of the Vice Chancellor about each of the matters covered in his judgment.
>
> Like the Vice Chancellor I shall assume that this final issue is properly described as mitigation rather than the assessment of damage. The plaintiff's claim is confined to damage suffered because she could not use her own car while it was being repaired. Such claims are commonplace. Assuming that there is indeed any loss (as to which, see Lord Mustill's warning in *Giles* v *Thompson* [1994] 1 AC 142, at 167, that "The need for a replacement car is not self-proving"), it is conventionally assessed by reference to the cost of hiring a substitute car while necessary repairs are carried out. The conventional approach is neither fixed nor immutable . . . Indeed if the approach were fixed or immutable Lord Mustill would not have expressed himself as he did in *Giles* v *Thompson*.
>
> What matters is that judges should look carefully at claims for hiring, both as to their duration and as to their rate. This will do much to avoid the inflated claims of which defendants' insurers are understandably apprehensive and will also discourage promotion of over optimistic claim by motorists . . . . .
>
> . . . It is therefore not possible to pronounce authoritatively and finally on the substantial practical question which concerns the present defendant's insurers, that is, whether it is reasonable for every plaintiff whose car has been damaged in circumstances in which the defendant's liability is obvious, or virtually so, to take advantage of the useful facilities offered by organisations such as 1st Automotive Limited. Without attempting to define the factual issues which may arise in any individual case the assessment will reflect ordinary questions such as the reasonableness of the use of an alternative vehicle, and appropriate steps to be taken in mitigation by the plaintiff. The circumstances are bound to vary. The individual plaintiff may have an urgent need immediately to find a replacement car, which may make it entirely reasonable for him to take advantage of the facilities offered by 1st Automotive Limited, or similar organisations, notwithstanding that the cost of the replacement vehicle would also include the additional expense necessary for these organisations to operate their businesses at a reasonable profit. Where the defendant's insurers are unwilling, or hesitate to accept liability in an obvious case, it may similarly be reasonable for the plaintiff to elect to use such services. On the other hand if the defendant's insurers make a rapid offer to provide an alternative vehicle, or to the limited extent of the damage actually sustained by the vehicle enables the plaintiff to use it while making reasonable enquiries to check on the alternatives, rather than simply involve the defendant (or his insurers) in an increased liability, it may be inappropriate to use the cost charged by

organisations like 1st Automotive as the correct basis for quantifying the claim for loss of use.

Reduced to a single word, the test is reasonableness, and where the claim is inflated it should be reduced to reasonable levels. Without attempting to define a disquisition on the relevant legal principles, in practical terms in most cases it may be useful for the actual rate of hiring an alternative vehicle to be taken as the normal starting point. If this figure represents local hire rates there is unlikely to be much dispute. If the alternative vehicle was hired from an organisation like 1st Automotive Limited, then if the defendant's insurers contend that this rate is unreasonable, they should be prepared to advance evidence, and argument. If the amount in dispute between the parties justifies the expense of litigation, the trial judge will have to assess the claim for loss of use in the light of his findings of fact.

Applying these principles to the present case, my preliminary view on reading the papers, and indeed during the course of argument, was that the judge's assessment in this present case was somewhat over-generous. The plaintiff, who had no urgent need of the replacement car, made no enquiries of the local rates available from hire companies, nor of the defendant's insurers, to check whether they would have been prepared to agree such rates. However, given that this was a question of fact for the trial judge, I am not prepared to dissent from the conclusion reached by the Vice Chancellor.

The House of Lords

A majority of the House of Lords disagreed with the majority view of the Court of Appeal on this issue.

Lord Hoffman stated that this issue "can be said to be the most important point on which your Lordships heard argument". It also transpired to be the most controversial. Lords Browne-Wilkinson, Hoffman and Hobhouse concluded that only "spot" hire rates could be recoverable, Lord Nicholls stated that the full rates should be recoverable and Lord Saville abstained on the point.

As mentioned above, the views expressed were not strictly necessary for dismissing the appeal and were arguably obiter. Indeed, Lord Saville in abstaining from the issue stated that the issue:

> does not arise for decision in the present case. This is a question of great importance and difficulty, the answer to which may well have widespread ramifications. It is accordingly a question that I would prefer to consider in a case where it does arise for decision.

This potentially let the door open for the issue to be re-argued at a later date in a different case. However the practice since then has been to treat *Dimond* as definitive. It may also suggest that there are relevant issues (perhaps such as the ones mentioned in this Chapter) which simply weren't argued in *Dimond.*

Nevertheless, at the very least the opinions will constitute very persuasive authority when the issue comes before the courts in other cases. The speeches in this case are interesting, particularly since there are subtle differences between the reasoning of two of the majority, Lords Hoffman and Hobhouse. Later in the Chapter, analysis will be made as to how these decisions may possibly lead to alternative attempts to recover any uplift.

a. Lords Hoffman and Browne Wilkinson
Lord Hoffman, with whom Lord Browne Wilkinson agreed, stated:

> My Lords, I would accept the judge's finding that Mrs. Dimond acted reasonably in going to 1st Automotive and availing herself of its services . . . She cannot therefore be said not to have taken reasonable steps to mitigate her damage.

> But that does not necessarily mean that she can recover the full amount charged by 1st Automotive. By virtue of her contract, she obtained not only the use of the car but additional benefits as well.

He described the additional benefits at pages 16 and 17:

i.   *credit charge:* "She was relieved of the necessity of laying out the money to pay for the car"; "providing credit to the hirers";

ii.   *costs of the action:* "She was relieved of the risk of having to bear the irrecoverable costs of successful litigation and the risk, small though it might be, of having to bear the expense of unsuccessful litigation"; "the irrecoverable costs of conducting the claim"; "Paying commission to brokers"; "checking that the accident was not the hirer's fault".

iii.   *possibly avoiding a residual liability:* "Depending upon the view one takes of the terms of agreement, she may have been relieved of the possibility of having to pay for the car at all."

iv.   *relieving the anxiety of the claim:* "She was relieved of the trouble and anxiety of pursuing a claim against Mr. Lovell or the C.I.S."

At page 16, he stated:

> My Lords, English law does not regard the need for any of these additional
> services as compensatable loss. As Sir Richard Scott V.-C. said (at [1999] 3
> W.L.R. 561, 580) "damages for worry and for the nuisance caused by
> having to deal with the consequences of an accident are not recoverable." If
> Mrs. Dimond had borrowed the hire money, paid someone else to conduct
> the claim on her behalf and insured herself against the risk of losing and any
> irrecoverable costs, her expenses would not have been recoverable. But the
> effect of the award of damages is that Mrs. Dimond has obtained
> compensation for them indirectly because they were offered as part of a
> package by 1st Automotive. There is in my opinion something wrong with
> this conclusion.

He then referred to the cases of *British Westinghouse Electric and
Manufacturing Co. Ltd.* v. *Underground Electric Railways Co. of London
Ltd* [1912] A.C. 673 and *Bellingham* v. *Dhillon* [1973] Q.B. 304 which
emphasised that only compensatory damages were recoverable. In other
words, additional benefits received whilst mitigating loss should not be taken
into account in quantifying the claim.

> How does one calculate the additional benefits that Mrs. Dimond received
> by choosing the 1st Automotive package to mitigate the loss caused by the
> accident to her car? . . . I do not think that a court can ignore the fact that,
> one way or another, the other benefits have to be paid for . . . How does one
> estimate the value of these additional benefits that Mrs. Dimond obtains? . .
> . I quite accept that a determination of the value of the benefits which must
> be brought into account will depend upon the facts of each case. But the
> principle to be applied is that in the *British Westinghouse* case [1912] A.C.
> 673 and this seems to me to lead to the conclusion that in the case of a
> hiring from an accident hire company, the equivalent spot rate will
> ordinarily be the net loss after allowance has been made for the additional
> benefits which the accident hire company has provided.

Potentially, Lord Hoffmann may have been quoting *British Westinghouse* on
the basis that the only service that 1st Automotive were technically obliged
to provide was the provision of a hire car. He had already found that they
were not under a duty to provide the other services. On that basis, the
Claimant would effectively have been getting the hire car at a rate above spot
hire and then the extra services for free. This being the case, she could only
have the reasonable spot hire rate for the hire and could have nothing for the
additional benefits since technically, they were provided free.

This left it open to Claimants to attempt to distinguish *Dimond* on the basis
either that the credit hire company was under a contractual duty to provide
the services or that the credit hire company intended to enforce the charges

against the Claimant. These attempts failed. *Dimond* is now seen as definitive.

b. Lord Hobhouse

On the face of it, Lord Hoffman made a similar analysis. He also decided that Mrs Dimond had acted reasonably and went on to emphasise the additional benefits. He described these at pages 19 and 23 as:

    i.   *credit charge*: "It is financing the transaction until the expected recovery is made from the other party"; "some element of interest";

    ii.   *costs of the action*: "it is bearing the cost of handling the claim and effecting that recovery"; "something in respect of costs".

    iii.   *possibly avoiding a residual liability*: "it is bearing a commercial (though not normally the legal) risk that there may be a failure to make that recovery".

However, his further analysis differed from that of Lord Hoffman. He favoured "the approach of making a commercial apportionment between the cost of hiring a car and the cost of the other benefits included in the scheme."

He was very careful in explaining that Mrs Dimond would not have been able to recover the whole cost "as the cost of mitigating the loss of use of her car". He said later, "The elements to which the uplift in the charges of the accident hire company was attributable were (and inevitably must be) elements which were not properly included in the claim for damages for loss of use."

In other words, the claim for the uplift was not recoverable in the claim for loss of use. This may possibly leave open the possibility that it may be recoverable in other ways. Indeed, this is possibly supported by his statement that "As appears from what I have said, some might be recovered from the wrongdoer in another form".

In any event, any such compensation in another form would probably be subject to two limitations. First, the Claimant would not be able to recover for the same thing twice:

> The necessity to make some apportionment or other reduction in the claim is demonstrated by the need to avoid double counting. Prima facie, the court should award statutory interest on the claim; but here the claim already

included some element of interest. Similarly the claim included something in respect of costs; to award costs as well would involve some duplication.

Second, Lord Hobhouse stated that, "it is unlikely that any scheme could be devised which would enable the insurance element to be recovered". By this he may well mean the possibility of avoiding a residual liability.

The heart of the difference between Lord Hoffmann and Lord Hobhouse is this: Lord Hoffmann thought that the measure of the Claimant's recoverable loss would simply be the equivalent spot hire rate while Lord Hobhouse seemed to prefer an approach based on stripping out the unrecoverable additional benefits from the credit hire charges. It is Lord Hoffmann's approach which has found favour in practice.

c. Lord Nicholls
The dissenting speech of Lord Nicholls was less ambiguous and simply suggested that the uplift should be recoverable. He described the "additional services" on page 2 as:

i. *credit charge*: "The hirer does not have to produce any money . . . at the time of the hiring";

ii. *costs of the action*: "The hire company pursues the allegedly negligent driver's insurers"; "The hire company is not deterred by having to bring court proceedings should this become necessary";

iii. *possibly avoiding a residual liability*: "The hirer does not have to produce any money, either at the time of the hiring or at all"; "If the claim is unsuccessful, in practice the hire company does not pursue the hirer".

He went on:

The additional services . . . redress the imbalance between the individual car owner and the insurance companies. They enable car owners to shift from themselves to the insurance companies a loss which properly belongs to the insurers but which, in practice, owners of cars often have to bear themselves. So long as the charge for the additional services is reasonable, this charge should be part of the recoverable damages.

A measure of damages which does not achieve this result would be sadly deficient. The law on the measure of damages should reflect the practicalities of the situation in which a wronged person finds himself. Otherwise it would mean that the law's response to a wrong is a right to damages which will often be illusory in practice. I do not believe this can be the present state of the law in a situation which affects thousands of people every year.

In *Burdis* v *Livsey*, at paragraphs 134 and 135 the Court of Appeal accepted without question the majority view of the House of Lords that only spot rates were recoverable. This makes it very difficult for Claimants to successfully distinguish *Dimond*. The clear position is that unless an exception applies, only spot hire rates are recoverable.

How to measure the Spot Hire Rate?

Having accepted that only the spot hire rate was recoverable, the Court of Appeal in *Burdis* then had to consider how to quantify the spot hire rate. The difficulty is that hire rates are in constant flux. They vary depending on the season and depending on the availability of particular vehicles. Furthermore the rates charged by different companies may vary considerably. Thus there is no single spot rate as such.

At first instances the Judge considered three ways of arriving at the right measure of damages:

> 1. Analysing the charges made by the credit hire company to uncover which charges related to irrecoverable additional benefits and which simply related to hiring the car. Both he and the Court of Appeal considered that this approach was too "cumbersome" to apply. It would lead to disproportionate costs and lengthy disclosure exercises.

> 2. Applying an arbitrary "reasonable discount" to the credit hire charges. The Court of Appeal also dismissed this approach, "we do not believe it appropriate in the absence of agreement between the parties or without cogent evidence as to what the discount should be. Further, as the judge pointed out, once the courts start applying a particular discount the total charge may be increased."

> 3. Considering the actual hire rates locally. This creates its own difficulties such as what companies to survey and whether to take the highest or the lowest rate. With some modifications as to the detail, this was the route which was eventually approved.

In the case, the Judge was assisted by expert evidence on rates provided by Mr Mainz and Mr McLean. Both had carried out surveys of the rates available in a particular area. The Mainz report in particular resulted in a band of rates. The Judge concluded that a band was no use. A single figure was needed. He was also concerned that the survey was a snapshot of rates at the time of the survey, which was January. The actual hire period was in peak season. Accordingly the first instance Judge adopted a rough and ready approach of Mainz plus 10%.

The Court of Appeal rejected this approach. They held:

> 146 ...That cannot be right. A person who needs to hire a car because of the negligence of another must, subject to mitigating his loss, be entitled to recover the actual cost of hire not an average derived from the Mainz report. If the principle adopted by the judge is correct then it would seem appropriate also to apply that principle to the cost of car repair, namely a claimant may only recover the average of the charges of garages. But a person whose car is damaged should in appropriate circumstances recover the cost to him of repair and loss of use. His recovery should not be restricted to an average of car repair or hire rates nor should he be able to recover that average cost if the actual cost is less. We believe that the solution is to apply normal legal principles.

> 147. The fundamental principle is that a person whose car has been damaged is entitled to compensation for the loss caused. In a case where such loss includes loss of use and he establishes a need for a replacement, he is entitled to the cost of hiring a replacement car. He can go round to the nearest car hire company and is prima facie entitled to recover the amount charged whether or not the charge is at the top of the range of car hire rates. However the basic principle is qualified by the duty to take reasonable steps to mitigate the loss. What is reasonable will depend on the particular circumstances.

> 148. We do not anticipate that the application of the correct legal principles will lead to disproportionate costs in small cases. The claim will be based on evidence as to the rate charged by a car hire company in the relevant area. Perhaps the rate will be at the top end of the range of company rates. Thereafter the evidential burden passes to the insurers to show that it would not have been reasonable to use that particular car hire company and that the reasonable course would be to use another company which charged a lower rate. What is reasonable and whether a loss is avoidable are questions of fact, not law, which District and County Court judges regularly decide. It can arise in many different types of cases, ranging from damage to chattels to a failure to take action. We do not believe that a decision on such issues in respect of car hire charges will be any more difficult than in respect of car repair charges.

How do the courts measure the recoverable element of the Claimant's loss? The simple answer according to *Burdis* v *Livsey* is to find evidence of the rate charged by a car hire company in the relevant area. Further it is not appropriate for the court to rely on averages – the answer must be based on an actual car hire rate not an average.

Remaining Rates Disputes

If the Court of Appeal in *Burdis* intended to lay down clear guidelines that would reduce the volume of credit hire litigation, they failed miserably. Rates based arguments are still run in the County Courts every day. In the following paragraphs I set out the most prevalent rates arguments.

Burden of Proof

Most County Courts appear to accept that the burden of proof rests on the Defendant to prove the rate charged by spot hire companies in the relevant area. This appears logical because after all it is the Defendant who is arguing for a reduction in the rate.

However, it is arguable that this is not what the Court of Appeal intended in *Burdis* v *Livsey*. At paragraph 148, which is the critical section of the Judgment, the first substantive statement reads "The claim will be based on evidence as to the rate charged by a car hire company in the relevant area". Claimants usually argue that all this requires them to do is to prove the rate charged by the credit hire company.

Defendants may point out that this section of the case is concerned only with ascertaining the spot hire rate. It applies where Claimants are not impecunious and hence there is no question of the credit hire rate being recovered in full. Therefore they argue it is for the Claimant, as part of proving their loss, to provide evidence of at least one spot hire rate.

The judgment continues "Thereafter the evidential burden passes to the insurers". Again, the use of the word thereafter suggests that the burden of proof only passes to the Defendant once the Claimant has first provided evidence of a spot hire rate.

Claimants may argue that the usual position with arguments of mitigation of loss is that the burden of proof rests on the Defendant. However the Defendant's answer is that this is not an argument about mitigation of loss but an argument about betterment. This point has been rather confused by the words of Lord Hope at paragraph 34 in *Lagden* v *O'Connor* [2004] 1 AC 1067: "It is for the defendant who seeks a deduction from expenditure in mitigation on the ground of betterment to make out his case for doing so." This appears to confuse issues of mitigation and betterment.

Locality

There may be a difference in the charges offered by national car hire chains and smaller local concerns. In general, the evidence before the Court of Appeal was that the national companies tend to be more expensive. Further different rates may be charged in different parts of the country.

What matters is that the evidence of car hire rates must be local to the Claimant. To use the Court of Appeal's words, it must be "in the relevant area". In part the reason for this is fairness, in that it avoids the possibility of manipulation of the figures by choosing rates evidence from a cheaper area. The main reason however is that the evidence must be from a company that the Claimant could have used.

Time / Seasonality

Claimants tend to hire vehicles within a short period of time after an accident. By the time the case reaches the courts, months or even years may have elapsed. Thus the rates evidence will never be contemporaneous with the actual hire period.

This is a matter of concern for Claimants. They argue that the car hire market is in constant flux. This fluctuation can sometimes be substantial. Rates are partly seasonal. At busy times of year the prices are higher. In truth the market is not driven so much by holiday traffic so as to be busy during the Summer months, but by the needs of corporations who hire large numbers of vehicles for their fleets.

Rates also vary depending on availability. If a car hire company has plenty of a particular car in stock, the price will be lower than if the car has to be sourced from elsewhere. If there is a shortage of a particular car on the rental market at any one time, then naturally the price will be higher.

There is a further concern about availability. Records are rarely obtainable years after the event to confirm whether a particular car hire company had a car available at the time to suit the Claimant's needs. The most that can usually be said is that the car hire company were in business at the time and had a similar car on their fleet.

This leads Claimants to argue that any rates evidence cannot be relied on. It can never be confirmed whether the specific vehicles quoted were available at the relevant time. Further the price of the vehicle at the relevant time can never be ascertained. Claimants may support this argument by reference to *Lagden* v *O'Connor* [2004] 1 AC 1067 at paragraph 34:

> It is for the defendant who seeks a deduction from expenditure in mitigation on the ground of betterment to make out his case for doing so. It is not enough that an element of betterment can be identified. It has to be shown that the claimant had a choice, and that he would have been able to mitigate his loss at less cost.... So if the evidence shows that the claimant had a choice, and that the route to mitigation which he chose was more costly than an alternative that was open to him, then a case will have been made out for a deduction. But if it shows that the claimant had no other choice available to him, the betterment must be seen as incidental to the step which he was entitled to take in the mitigation of his loss and there will be no ground for it to be deducted.

Claimants may rely on this to argue that unless the Defendant can show that there was a cheaper alternative available locally at the time of the hire period, then the Defendant has failed to prove that the Claimant had a choice.

Defendants may argue in response that they are providing the best evidence that is available. It just is not possible to obtain evidence about the time that the Claimant hired. The Court of Appeal cannot have intended to set Defendants an impossible task. Arguments about proportionality will also be relevant, especially in small claims cases.

Defendants may also argue that availability is not relevant at all. The issue is one of betterment. The court's task is to identify what it would rate the Claimant would have been willing to pay a spot hire company. On this analysis the question of availability simply does not arise. Furthermore the effect of relying on availability arguments is to "ignore" the fact that additional benefits have been incurred (*c.f.* Lord Hoffmann in *Dimond* at page 402).

Expert / Lay

One argument that often arises is whether the rates evidence is properly classed as expert evidence or lay evidence. Evidentially the crucial difference is that an expert witness may give opinion evidence. The point can arise in a number of ways. Defendants may seek to argue that their rates evidence is expert to lend it extra authority or to allow their witness to answer questions with their opinion. By contrast, particularly on the small claims track where the courts are reluctant to give permission for expert evidence, the Claimant may argue that the rates evidence is expert and should be excluded.

The point is arguable either way. It is noted however that Colin McLean was allowed to give expert evidence in *Burdis*.

Both sides should seek to use this to gain a tactical advantage. Defendants should seek permission in allocation questionnaires to instruct expert evidence. Claimants should seek to argue that no expert evidence is required.

Methodology

Claimants also attack the methodology of the rates survey in many ways, including:-

> a) the rates may not be comparable with the rate offered by the credit hire company. In particular there may be a much higher excess or insurance charge, or there may be additional terms such as limited mileage. There may also be a substantial deposit required up front.

> b) the rate may be based on a discount for the number of days hired. The Claimant will not know at the start of the hire period how long he needs the hire vehicle for. This may lead to him being charged a higher rate.

> c) the person obtaining the rates evidence may be a specialist in carrying out these surveys. They may therefore be in a better position than the Claimant would have found himself in. It is important to check whether the rates evidence was obtained by looking up car hire companies in the local yellow pages rather than by using companies known to the surveyor.

> d) the Claimant will want the person who actually carried out the survey to attend for cross examination – it is arguably not good enough for on person to carry out the survey and for another person to write up the report and give evidence.

ABI Rates

It is not appropriate for Defendants to rely upon ABI Rates. As the Court of Appeal said in *Burdis* at paragraph 150:

> No doubt the scheme is, and will be, of benefit to insurers, the accident hire companies and the public; but the ABI figures cannot be taken in hostile

litigation as being the appropriate figures of loss. They reflect a compromise agreed between the parties rather than an assessment of loss.

The simple truth is that the ABI Rates and the General Terms of Agreement are not relevant to the court's task in these cases. They will be left out of account.

Internet Rates

A recent development is that Defendants have sought to rely on rates evidence obtained from the internet, either by way of print outs from car hire websites or from databases. The advantage to the Defendant is that this is cheaper than commissioning a report and in a small claim the evidence may be adduced without needing a witness to attend.

In *Smith v Burney* (27 April 2007 unreported) the Claimant appealed a decision by a District Judge to admit internet rates evidence which was served late and without a witness attending to adduce it. The court upheld the decision to admit the evidence. Firstly, the case was a small claim and the strict rules of evidence did not apply. Secondly, the evidence spoke for itself and it did not need cross-examination to comment on the weaknesses in it. Thirdly, the evidence was easily verifiable. The result is that internet rates evidence is likely to be used increasing in low value cases.

Chapter 9

IMPECUNIOSITY

The House of Lords decision in *Dimond* v *Lovell* left one important argument open to Claimants. It is one thing, so the argument runs, to say that a Claimant who can afford to do so should avail himself of spot hire rates. But this does not address the position of the impecunious Claimant. Such a Claimant could not afford to spot hire and so does not have a choice between credit hire and spot hire: it is credit hire or nothing. Should an impecunious Claimant therefore be able to recover the full cost of a credit hire vehicle including the additional charges?

The issue went to the House of Lords in *Lagden* v *O'Connor* [2004] 1 AC 1067. *Lagden* was one of the four other cases heard together by the Court of Appeal along with *Burdis* v *Livsey*. In the Court of Appeal the Claimant had been allowed to recover the credit hire charges in full. The Defendant appealed to the House of Lords. By a 3 – 2 majority the House of Lords upheld the Court of Appeal.

The facts

The Defendant, Ms O'Connor, had driven into Mr Lagden's parked Ford Granada, causing it damage. Mr Lagden took his car to the garage to be repaired. He was unemployed and in poor health. He had very little money and could not afford to pay for a hire car while his own was off the road.

Accordingly, Mr Lagden entered into a credit hire contract with Helphire to hire a Ford Mondeo while his own vehicle was unusable. The total cost was £659.76. This cost included sums which would ordinarily not be recoverable by virtue of *Dimond* v *Lovell*.

The majority verdict

Lord Hope delivered the most detailed of the three speeches in the majority. He described the problem thus, at paragraph 30:

> But what if the injured party has no choice? What if the only way that is open to him to minimise his loss is by expending money which results in an

incidental and additional benefit which he did not seek but the value of which can nevertheless be identified? Does the law require gain to be balanced against loss in these circumstances? If it does, he will be unable to recover all the money that he had to spend in mitigation. So he will be at risk of being worse off than he was before the accident. That would be contrary to the elementary rule that the purpose of an award of damages is to place the injured party in the same position as he was before the accident as nearly as possible.

He reviewed the authorities and concluded at paragraph 34:

> But what if the injured party has no choice? What if the only way that is open to him to minimise his loss is by expending money which results in an incidental and additional benefit which he did not seek but the value of which can nevertheless be identified? Does the law require gain to be balanced against loss in these circumstances? If it does, he will be unable to recover all the money that he had to spend in mitigation. So he will be at risk of being worse off than he was before the accident. That would be contrary to the elementary rule that the purpose of an award of damages is to place the injured party in the same position as he was before the accident as nearly as possible.

And at paragraph 37:

> But it is reasonably foreseeable that there will be some car owners who will be unable to produce an acceptable credit or debit card and will not have the money in hand to pay for the hire in cash before collection. In their case the cost of paying for the provision of additional services by a credit hire company must be attributed in law not to the choice of the motorist but to the act or omission of the wrongdoer. That is Mr Lagden's case. In law the money which he spent to obtain the services of the credit hire company is recoverable.

Lord Hope also rejected the Defendant's arguments based on *The Liesbosch* [1933] AC 449. In that case the House of Lords had held that the damages payable by a Defendant could not be increased by virtue of a Claimant's impecuniosity. Lord Hope stopped short of saying that *The Liesbosch* was wrongly decided. However, he said that the law had moved on. The present position is that a wrongdoer must take his victim as he finds him: this applies to the victim's economic state as well as to his physical vulnerability.

The other two majority speeches were shorter. Lord Nicholls (with whom Lord Slynn agreed) attacked the case from a common sense point of view:

> the law would be seriously defective if in this type of case the innocent motorist were in practice unable to obtain the use of a replacement car. The law does not assess damages payable to an innocent plaintiff on the basis

that he is expected to perform the impossible. The common law prides itself on being sensible and reasonable. It had regard to practical realities.

He continued:

Here, as elsewhere, a negligent driver must take his victim as he finds him. Common fairness requires that if an innocent plaintiff cannot afford to pay car hire charges, so that left to himself he would be unable to obtain a replacement car to meet the need created by the negligent driver, then the damages payable under this head of loss should include the reasonable costs of a credit hire company.

The minority view

We will set out more briefly the judgments given in the minority.

Lord Scott began at paragraph 81 by describing the type of loss involved:

the claim to recover the car- hire charges can be viewed simply as a claim to recover an item of special damages representing expenditure incurred as a result of the defendant's negligence. On that approach, however, recovery cannot be claimed simply on the basis that the expenditure was reasonably incurred by the injured party. It would, in principle, be necessary also to show that the expenditure reasonably or probably arose out of the defendant's negligence (see Martin B in *Prehn* v *Royal Bank of Liverpool*); in other words, the expenditure must have been reasonably foreseeable.

He continued that the criterion of "reasonable foreseeability" had overtaken other notions about special damages. In so doing he accepted what Lord Hope had said about *The Liesbosch.* However he continued that:

The majority decision in *Dimond* v *Lovell* did not bar recovery on the ground that the incurring of the higher car-hire charges was not reasonably foreseeable. It barred recovery on the ground that, in law, the cost of financing payment of the repairs bill and payment of the car hire charges and the cost of services in handling the damages claim could not, as a matter of law, constitute special damages claims. If reasonable forseeability had been the criterion, Mrs Dimond would have recovered the whole of the credit hire charges. Everyone, in the Court of Appeal and in this House, agreed that it had been reasonable for her to enter into the credit hire agreement. None of your Lordships on this appeal has suggested that the majority view in *Dimond* v *Lovell* was wrong.

It must follow, first, that reasonable forseeability may be a necessary but is not a sufficient criterion for the recovery of the full car hire charges, and, secondly, that your Lordships must approach this appeal on the footing, confirmed by *Dimond* v *Lovell*, that, in principle, the law will not permit the cost of financing a payment recoverable as special damages to be itself recoverable as special damages nor the cost of services in handling a damages claim to be recoverable as special damages."

Lord Scott then posed the question whether it would be desirable to create an exception to the rule in *Dimond*. He held that it would not. His reason was that it would not be practical to determine whether a person is impecunious. He dismissed the suggestion that possession of a credit card was a sufficient test, because people without credit cards might nevertheless have cash stashed in their houses or generous overdraft facilities.

Lord Walker also agreed that it was time to depart from *The Liesbosch*. However he disagreed with the majority both as a matter of principle and as a matter of practice. At paragraph 104 he said:

> As a matter of principle, it would not in my view be right to permit a claimant's impecuniosity, however much it may attract sympathy, to enable him to obtain compensation under a head which English law does not regard as part of his compensatable loss. This claimant's choice was restricted by his extreme impecuniosity. The freedom of choice open to other claimants might be restricted by all sorts of other circumstances, such as the remote geographical location in which an accident occurred, the specialised character of the claimant's vehicle, or a dislocation of the normal market caused by exceptional demand. The proposed modification of the principle in *Dimond* v *Lovell* seems dangerously open-ended.

He continued at paragraph 106:

> To my mind policy considerations point to the same conclusion. The concept of a claimant being unable to hire a replacement car (otherwise than through an accident hire company) because of impecuniosity is, as was acknowledged in the course of argument, a vague one. In practice, many claimants will go to an accident hire company if they can, simply because of its convenience, without asking themselves whether they could afford the alternative of hiring from a conventional car-hire firm; and if they do consider the alternative, the choice is likely to depend on temperament and resourcefulness, rather than on some minute calculation of their margin of solvency. To allow the exception would be liable to lead to an increase in contested small claims, contrary to the public interest.

How to define impecuniosity?

As set out above one of the principal concerns of the minority was the difficulty in defining impecuniosity. This has the most resonance in practice today. How then did the majority define impecuniosity?

Lord Nicholls stated at paragraph 9 that:

> There remains the difficult point of what is meant by 'impecunious' in the context of the present type of case. Lack of financial means is, almost always, a question of priorities. In the present context what it signifies is inability to pay car hire charges without making sacrifices the plaintiff could not reasonably be expected to make. I am fully conscious of the open-ended nature of this test. But fears that this will lead to increased litigation in small claims courts seem to me exaggerated. It is in the interests of all concerned to avoid litigation with its attendant costs and delay. Motor insurers and credit hire companies should be able to agree on standard enquiries, or some other means, which in practice can most readily give effect to this test of impecuniosity.

Lord Hope expressed himself rather less concisely. He began at paragraphs 36 – 37:

> In practice, for reasons that are obvious, companies which offer cars for hire in the open market insist on payment of the rental up front before the car is collected, together with a sum to cover the risk of damage to the car while it is on hire. Payment is usually made by means of a credit card or a debit card. Some companies may accept cash, but if they do the sum that will have to be paid up front will not be small. Many car owners are, of course, well able to provide what is needed to satisfy the hirer that the money which is needed to pay for the hire is available. If they choose to use the services of a credit hire company they must accept as a deduction from their expenditure the extra cost of doing so. The full cost of obtaining the services of a credit hire company cannot be claimed by the motorist who is able to pay the cost of the hire up front without exposing himself or his family to a loss or burden which is unreasonable.

> But it is reasonably foreseeable that there will be some car owners who will be unable to produce an acceptable credit or debit card and will not have the money in hand to pay for the hire in cash before collection. In their case the cost of paying for the provision of additional services by a credit hire company must be attributed in law not to the choice of the motorist but to the act or omission of the wrongdoer.

He returned to the theme at paragraphs 41 – 42:

> There is another consideration which must be mentioned. We cannot ignore the fact that accidents of the kind that befell Mr Lagden's motor car happen every day. There are thousands of such claims, most of which are of very small value and not worth the cost of litigating. It is in nobody's interest that these cases should be forced into court where there is no issue about liability. Everything points to reducing the opportunity for dispute to a minimum so that they can be settled out of court at minimum cost as soon as possible. It was largely with a view to achieving this object that this series

of test cases was brought before the courts by the motor insurance companies. It is suggested that the benefits that were achieved by the decision in *Dimond* v *Lovell* will be set aside if an exception were to be made in favour of the impecunious. The adjective is incapable of precise definition. Case after case, it is said, will have to come to court in order to resolve the issue whether the claimant had no choice but to use the services of a credit hire company.

The Court of Appeal was alive to this issue. In its judgment, at p 83, para 128, the court said:

> "We realise that in some cases it will be necessary to consider the financial ability of a claimant to pay car hire charges. However we do not anticipate that district and county court judges will not be able to arrive at a just result without putting the parties to great expense."

That seems to me to be a fair assessment. In practice the dividing line is likely to lie between those who have, and those who do not have, the benefit of a recognised credit or debit card. It ought to be possible to identify those cases where the selection has been made on grounds of convenience only without much difficulty."

The test most widely adopted appears to be that of unreasonable burden / sacrifice. However it remains open to Defendants to argue that mere possession of a credit / debit card is enough to render a Claimant pecunious.

Practical implications

The minority in the House of Lords were right to be concerned about the effects of this decision upon credit hire litigation. Claimants now routinely argue impecuniosity. The benefits of succeeding on this argument are obvious: they recover the full credit hire rate. The imprecise nature of the test leaves it entirely open for different District Judges to arrive at different conclusions. Ultimately of course, whether a person is impecunious is a question of fact to be determined at the hearing. The burden of proof lies with the Claimant.

Defendants may well ask at an early stage whether impecuniosity is in issue. If it is, searching questions may be put to the Claimant to inquire about his savings, earnings and availability of credit / debit cards. It is also perfectly proper for Defendants, even in small claims, to seek disclosure of the Claimants current account bank statements for the hire period (and possibly for longer). This will entail astute use of both Part 18 Questions and requests for disclosure.

Other points at the fringes of impecuniosity remain to be resolved. For example, how far is the court entitled to take account of the earnings of the Claimant's partner in determining impecuniosity? In this context, the case of *Fettes* v *Williams* (22 January 2003) is interesting because HHJ Hull QC was quite prepared to take account of the Claimant's husband's earnings in deciding that she was not impecunious.

Another point which often arises in County Court hearings is how far the Defendant is allowed to go in cross examination of the Claimant. Is it proper to ask questions about whether the Claimant could take a payment holiday on their mortgage, although this might put their house at risk. Defendants may argue that this is a proper question because the issue is whether the Claimant could have afforded to hire not whether it would have been sensible for them to do so. Claimants may argue that such questions become disproportionate.

Other Exceptions to Dimond?

The majority judgments in *Lagden* are based on the premise that the impecunious Claimant has no choice but to hire from a credit hire company. Might there be other Claimants who are unable to hire from a spot hire company?

It is sometimes argued that the Claimant's age is relevant. Many spot hire companies will not hire a vehicle to a Claimant who is under 21. Claimants may potentially argue that such a person has no choice but to hire on credit. The same arguments might apply to a Claimant with a number of previous convictions for driving offences.

Claimants also argue *Lagden* in relation to rates. They point out that the burden of proof on rates evidence must be on the Defendant because the Defendant has to show that the Claimant had a choice between spot and credit hire (*c.f.* Lord Hope at paragraph 34).

The Defendant's response might be to argue that *Lagden* is a narrow decision focussing on the question of impecuniosity alone. Throughout their speeches their Lordships were focussing only on the question of financial means. It is therefore misleading, it might be argued, to submit that the judgement has any wider implications: instead, it might be said, that it creates one narrow exception only.

Chapter 10

MITIGATION OF LOSS

With the decline in consumer credit points, the issue of mitigation has taken on increased importance in recent years.

Burden of Proof

It is axiomatic that Claimants must take reasonable steps to mitigate their loss. This is frequently referred to as the duty to mitigate. However as we shall see this is not strictly accurate, the Claimant being under no actual duty.

It is equally clear that the Defendant bears the burden of proving that the Claimant has failed to mitigate their loss.

Standard of Mitigation

The standard of mitigation has been expressed in different terms from time to time. Claimants will rely on the purple prose of Lord MacMillan in *Banco de Portugal* v *Waterlow and Sons Ltd* [1932] AC 452, 506:

> Where the sufferer from a breach of contract finds himself in consequence of that breach placed in a position of embarrassment the measures which he may be driven to adopt in order to extricate himself ought not to be weighed in nice scales at the instance of the party whose breach of contract has occasioned the difficulty. It is often easy after an emergency has passed to criticise the steps which have been taken to meet it, but such criticism does not come well from those who have themselves created the emergency. The law is satisfied if the party placed in the difficult by reason of the breach of a duty owed to him has acted reasonably in the adoption of remedial measures and he will not be held disentitled to recover the cost of such measures merely because the party in breach can suggest that other measures less burdensome to him have been taken.

Of course Lord MacMillan was speaking specifically about breach of contract. However his comments apply equally to tort. This was affirmed (for example) by Nourse LJ in *Mattocks* v *Mann* 1993 RTR 13 at 21E,

Davies LJ in *Moore v DER* [1971] 1 WLR 1476 and in *McGregor on Damages.*

Defendants may also point to the following:

> The person who has broken the contract is not to be exposed to additional cost by reason of the plaintiffs not doing what they ought to have done as reasonable men, and the plaintiffs not being under any obligation to do anything otherwise than in the ordinary course of business." James L.J. in *Dunkirk Colliery Co. v Lever* (1878) 9 Ch.D.20, 25. Cited with approval by Viscount Haldane in *British Westinghouse Electric and Manufacturing Co. Ltd v Underground Electric Railways Company of London Ltd* [1912] AC 673 (at 689.)

> For the purposes of the present case it is important to appreciate the true nature of the so-called "duty to mitigate the loss" or duty to minimise the damage". The plaintiff is not under any actual obligation to adopt the cheaper method: if he wishes to adopt the more expensive method he is at liberty to do so and by doing so commits no wrong against the defendant or anyone else. The true meaning is that the plaintiff is not entitled to charge the defendant by way of damages with any greater sum than that which he reasonably needs to expend for the purpose of making good the loss. In short, he is fully entitled to be as extravagant as he pleases but not at the expense of the Defendant...

> "In my view it is impossible to find from the evidence that the plaintiff took all reasonable steps to mitigate the loss, or did all that he reasonably could to keep down the cost. He was fully entitled to have his damaged vehicle repaired at whatever cost because he preferred it. But he was not justified in charging against the defendant the cost of repairing the damaged vehicle when that cost was more than twice the replacement market value and he had made no attempt to find a replacement vehicle.
> Pearson LJ in Derbyshire v Warren [1963] 1 WLR 1067 at 1075.

Questions of mitigation are particularly prone to arise in the following contexts:-

1. Need for a Hire Car
2. Courtesy Cars
3. Like for Like
4. Period of Hire
5. Different Cars
6. Self-Employed Claimants

1. Need for a Hire Car

In *Giles* v *Thompson*, Lord Mustill also gave useful guidance regarding proof of the need for a hire car in the first place. He stated that "the need for a replacement car is not self-proving." However, in the next sentence, he continued:

> The motorist may have been in hospital throughout . . . ; or he may have been planning to go abroad for a holiday leaving his car behind; and so on. . . . I agree with the Court of Appeal that it is not hard to infer that a motorist who incurs the considerable expense of running a private car does so because he has a need for it, and consequently has a need to replace it if, as a result of a wrongful act, it is put out of commission.

He went on to say that it was for the Defendant to "displace the inference" which otherwise arose. In the Court of Appeal, Steyn LJ had used similar examples to Lord Mustill for circumstances in which a Defendant might prove that there was no need to hire a car. He used the example of hiring a car in the United Kingdom when the Claimant was abroad (at page 337H) and said that the Claimant "clearly" did not have to show that the car was "essential" (at page 337J).

However, Lord Mustill went on to warn against permitting exaggerated claims for car hire:

> What matters is that the judges should look carefully at claims for hiring, both as to their duration and as to their rate. This will do much to avoid the inflated claims of which the defendants' insurers are understandably apprehensive, and will also discourage the promotion of over-optimistic claims by motorists, who if the present forms of agreement are enforced in accordance with their terms may be left with residual liabilities for hiring charges. The discipline imposed by judges who have the acumen and experience to detect greed and slapdash claims procedures will in my opinion do much more to forestall abuse than a dusting-down of the old law of champerty.

He continued at pages 164 -165:

> And as to the possibility that the scheme will encourage motorists to hire cars which they do not need, at the ultimate expense of the insurers, I am confident that resourceful lawyers are well able to press by interlocutory measures for a candid exposure of the motorist's true requirements, and, if all else fails, to fight the issue at an oral hearing, as happened in the present case. If the motorists are found to have been tempted by the hire companies into the unnecessary hiring of substitute vehicles, the claims will fail pro tanto, with consequent orders for costs which will impose a healthy discipline upon the companies.

The position in practice is that while formally the need to hire a vehicle is not self-proving, it almost proves itself. Outside the given examples, where the Claimant is overseas or in hospital, it is difficult to imagine a situation in which a court would hold that a Claimant did not need a hire vehicle.

2. Courtesy cars

The issue here is simple: is it reasonable for a Claimant to hire a replacement vehicle where they have been offered a courtesy car either through their own insurance or by the Defendant?

From own Insurer
This issue has caused confusion and inconsistency in the County Courts. Defendants may point to *Callender* v *Ray Braidwood & Sons* [1999] 1 CL, *Bucknall* v *Jepson* [1998] CLY 1456, *Spence* v *United Taxis* [1998] CLY 1465 and *Ball* v *Howells Transport* [1999] CL, DJ Ackroyd and *Lyons* v *Metcalf* [1999] CLY 2494 where failure to take a courtesy car was held to constitute a failure to mitigate and hire charges were not recovered (save that in Lyons this was obiter since the claim failed in any event).

However Claimants may rely on *Perehenic* v *Deboa Structuring* [1998] CLY 1467 and *Cockburn* v *Davies and Provident Insurance Plc* [1997] CLY 1805 where failure to take a courtesy car was not held to have been a failure to mitigate and hire charges were awarded.

Claimants may argue that they are not obliged to use their insurance to benefit the Defendant. The starting point for this argument is *Parry* v *Cleaver* [1970] AC 1. This case is familiar to personal injury lawyers as it holds that payments that the Claimant has received from occupational disability pensions do not have to be deducted from his damages. It also establishes a more general principle. Lord Reid stated at page 14:

> As regards moneys coming to the plaintiff under a contract of insurance, I think that the real and substantial reason for disregarding them is that the plaintiff has bought them and that it would be unjust and unreasonable to hold that the money which he has prudently spent on premiums and the benefit from it should enure to the benefit of the tortfeasor. Here again I think that the explanation that this is too remote is artificial and unreal. Why should the plaintiff be left worse off than if he had never insured?

Claimants may further argue that not taking advantage of a courtesy car is not a failure to mitigate. This argument is bound to depend upon the facts: it may be relevant whether the Claimant's no claims bonus is under threat for example. However, in a credit hire context, *Martindale* v *Duncan* [1973] 1

WLR 547 may be cited. In that case, the Court of Appeal held that on the facts of that case it was not a failure to mitigate for the Claimant to seek to recover damages from the Defendant in the first instance rather than his own insurer. Davies LJ said at page 577:

> The plaintiff was seeking in the first instance to recover his damage from the defendant's insurers and, if anything went wrong with that claim, although he obviously would not want to forfeit his "no claims" bonus, the second string to his bow would be to recover the money from his own insurers, and until he had had authorisation for doing the work he could not be at all certain that he would stand in a good position *vis-a-vis* the insurance company.

The Court of Appeal went on to hold that it was not a failure to mitigate on the facts of that case for the Claimant to seek to recover damages in the first instance from the Defendant's insurers rather than claiming against his own insurers.

On a slightly different tack but reaching the same result, in *Seddon* v *Tekin* [2001] GCCR 2865 HHJ Harris stated that "There is no reason why a Defendant should be able to take advantage of the fact that the plaintiff is insured to reduce his own loss, and if the plaintiff did so by taking the car from his own insurer then his own insurer could recover the cost from the Defendant anyway, so the defendant's position would not be improved".

This line of authority was considered in *Rose* v *The Co-operative Group* 7 February 2005, in which the Circuit Judge concluded "whether or not the Claimant knew or ought to have known he had a choice of car free of charge through his own insurance, the availability of such a choice by use of his own insurance should be disregarded."

Claimants may also refer to the judgment of Nicholson LJ in *McMullen* v *Gibney and Bibney* [1999] NIQB 1 (13 January 1999) sitting in the High Court of Northern Ireland, which also held that the availability of a courtesy car to a claimant under a policy of insurance afforded no defence to a claim for hire of a replacement vehicle.

A further argument for the Claimant derives from the case of the *Liverpool* (No 2) [1963] P64. In that case the Court of Appeal held that where the victim of an accident has differing and alternative rights for the same loss against a tortfeasor and against another in contract he is not required to take steps to recover his loss from the other party from whom he could recover in contract. Interestingly, the Court of Appeal indicated that their decision was nothing to do with mitigation. This suggests that this is a distinct argument.

For the moment the courtesy car argument looks like a difficult one for Defendants to run. The law has developed since the County Court cases (cited above) in which Judges found that not taking a courtesy car was a failure to mitigate and now favours Claimants.

From Defendant's Insurer

Where the offer of a car comes not from the Claimant's own insurers but is an offer of a free car from the Defendant's insurers, Defendants may seek to distinguish the above cases on the basis that this would not constitute availing oneself of a policy of insurance. In *Snashall* v *Colver* 8 February 2002, for example, the Judge said: "the Claimant cannot recover for avoidable loss". In that case a letter was sent to the Claimant directly offering him a courtesy car. The Judge held that this was a bona fide offer. On the facts it would have been reasonable for the Claimant to have accepted it.

The issue is not so straightforward however. Claimants may argue that the Defendant did not tell them the full terms and conditions of the offer. It may be that some more onerous term was lurking in the background, such that it would have been reasonable not to take the vehicle. Claimants may ask whether the Defendant would have offered a collision damage waiver or whether additional drivers would have been permitted. Also whether the Defendant would have offered an appropriate vehicle to the Claimant.

Fuchs Lubricants Plc v *Staybrite Windows Ltd* [1999] 10 CL is an example of a case where the Defendant's insurers had written to the Claimant prior to the commencement of the hire offering a courtesy car for free. The Judge found that the Claimant had acted reasonably in using the hire company rather than the Defendant's insurers to provide a replacement vehicle because the provision of a replacement vehicle by the Defendant's insurers would not have been free. It was said that a Defendant's insurer could not dictate which company should be used by an innocent party to supply a replacement vehicle, provided the charges sought were in line with those of other hire companies. The Claimant was awarded the hire charges in full.

Defendant insurers have also argued that sending a generic letter to credit hire companies offering a courtesy vehicle to their customers in the event of a car being damaged in a no fault accident can potentially give rise to a failure to mitigate. This was considered at first instance in *Bee* v *Jenson* [2006] EWHC 2534 by Cresswell J. The Defendant's argument was struck out on that occasion. Indeed part of the Defendant's case was described as "inaccurate, misleading and embarrassing". The reasons in that case were first that the Defendant insurer did not contact the Claimant directly.

Second, the letter in question was not precise enough to amount to an offer. It did not mention a specific vehicle or a specific period.

Suppose that the court finds that it was unreasonable for the Claimant not to accept the car offered by the Defendant insurer. Does this extinguish the Defendant's liability to the Claimant altogether or merely abate it. In *Evans* v *TNT Logistics Ltd* (unreported) the Claimant hired a replacement vehicle at a daily rate of £70. The Defendant insurer offered the Claimant a replacement vehicle at a cost of £29 per day, which they offered to meet. On appeal it was held to be unreasonable not to accept the vehicle offered by the Defendant. The Defendant argued that this meant the Claimant should recover nothing. The Judge however held that the Claimant could still recover £29 per day from the Defendant. He found that if the Claimant had hired an alternative vehicle at a lower cost than £29 per day, the Defendant could hardly argue that that was unreasonable. He was prepared to treat the offer of a vehicle worth £29 per day as analogous to an offer of money. The result is that the Claimant is able to recover the sum which he would have received had he acted reasonably, in this case £29 a day. It remains to be seen how other courts will react, presented with this argument.

3. Like for Like

Is a Claimant who drives a particular vehicle entitled to hire the same or an equivalent vehicle? Or should he, in mitigation of his loss, accept a lesser vehicle? The question often arises particularly in respect of Claimants who drive so called prestige cars such as BMWs or Mercedes.

Different cases have again reached inconsistent results on this point. Like for like was allowed or the principle assumed or accepted in: *Watson Norie Ltd* v *Shaw* [1967] 111 Sol Jo 117; *Mattocks* v *Mann* [1993] RTR 13; *H L Motorworks* v *Alwabi* [1977] RTR 276 (although, note that this case may potentially also be used to argue against like for like); *Daily Office Cleaning Contractors* v *Shefford* [1977] RTR 361; *Williams* v *Hoggins* [1996] CLY 2148 and *Vaughan Transport Systems* v *Fackrell* [1997] CLY 1810. However cases in which like for like hiring was held to be unreasonable include: *Lyne* v *Cawley* [1995] CLY 1624 and *Gowen* v *Owens Radio and TV* [1995] CLY 1631.

In *H L Motorworks* v *Alwabi*, a Rolls Royce was the vehicle damaged. Cairns LJ held that:

> On the face of it, the customer was entitled to have, during the 11 days for which he was deprived of his Rolls Royce, another Rolls Royce to take its place. If it could have been shown that the amount of use he wished to make

of the car in those 11 days was very small or that some other car would have been equally suitable for his purpose, then it may well be that the plaintiff company should not have met his full claim, or, if they did, would not have been entitled to pass on the claim to the defendant. But those matters, I apprehend, would be for the defendant to establish.

In *Burdis* v *Livsey*, the Court of Appeal concluded on this issue at paragraph 133: "if a need for a particular replacement car is established, then the cost incurred of hiring that car is recoverable." Defendants may say that this appears to place the burden of proof on the Claimant, at least to establish a prima facie case of need for a particular vehicle. Claimants may point to the very low threshold for establishing need mentioned by Lord Mustill in *Giles* v *Thompson* (cited at the start of this chapter).

The present consensus is that prima facie, it is not unreasonable for a Claimant to hire a car which is the same or equivalent to that which was damaged. However it is open for the Defendant to argue that this was unreasonable where the specific facts permit. Beyond this, when the courts are called upon to adjudicate on rates evidence they will often have to determine what represents an equivalent vehicle and evidence may well be led on this issue.

4. Period of hire

Defendants may sometimes argue that the period of hire was unreasonable and that they should not be responsible for paying for the whole of that period.

Delay by Garage
Where there has been delay on the part of a garage, Defendants used to rely on *Charnock* v *Liverpool Corporation* [1968] 1 WLR 1498, in which the Court of Appeal held that where the owner of a car took it to a garage for repair on the basis that the insurers would pay the cost of the repairs in pursuance of an estimate which they had accepted, the proper inference was that there was a contract between the car owner and garage to repair the car at a price acceptable to the insurers within a reasonable time and also a contract between the garage and the insurers. Accordingly, in that case, it was held that there was a contract between the Claimant and the Second Defendants to repair the car within a reasonable time. This was relied upon by HHJ Harris in *Clark* v *Ardington*.

However, in *Mattocks* v *Mann* [1973] RTR 13, the Court of Appeal had to consider a case in which there had been a delay in repairing the Claimant's car. Bedlam LJ giving the leading judgment held that: "For a supervening cause or a failure to mitigate to relieve a Defendant of a period of hire there must, in my judgment, be a finding of some conduct on her [Mrs Mattocks] part or on the part of someone for whom she is in law responsible, or indeed of a third party, which can truly be said to be an independent cause of loss of her car for that period."

In *Clark* v *Ardington*, the Court of Appeal approved the earlier decision in *Mattocks* and also a privy council decision *Candlewood Navigation Corporation Ltd* v *Mitsui O.S.K. Lines Ltd* [1986] 1 AC 1. The Court of Appeal concluded at paragraph 121:

> The defendants' actions damaged the cars of Mrs Clark and Mr Dennard. They should pay the loss caused by their actions. The actual loss incurred involved hire of replacement cars for 10 days in the case of Mrs Clark and 12 days in the case of Mr Dennard. They both appear to have acted reasonably in placing the cars in the hands of respectable repairers and there were no supervening events. Further delays of that order were foreseeable. The extra loss caused by the delay in the repair must fall on the tortfeasor as there was no failure to mitigate. On the findings of fact in those cases the cost of hire should not have been reduced. The insurers of the defendants should seek a contribution from the repairers for any unjustified length of repair.

Thus where the Claimant's car takes an unexpectedly long time to repair, the Defendant will remain liable for the whole hire period unless the Defendant can point to any failure to mitigate on the part of the Claimant, his servants or agents.

Claiming a Contribution from the Garage
Section 1(1) of the Civil Liability (Contribution) Act 1978 provides as follows:

> Subject to the following provisions of this section, any person liable in respect of any damage suffered by another person may recover contribution from any other person liable in respect of the same damage (whether jointly or otherwise).

Defendants may rely on this section to bring contribution proceedings against the repairing garage, where the garage has delayed in carrying out repairs. The important point procedurally is that the Defendant is alleging that the garage breached its duty of care / contract with the Claimant. This is significant because it is unlikely that the garage owes any duties to the Defendant directly.

What duty the garage owes to the Claimant is inevitably fact sensitive. However in *Charnock* v *Liverpool Corporation* [1968] 1 WLR 1498, the

Court of Appeal held that where the owner of a car took it to a garage for repair, on the basis that his insurers would pay the cost of the repairs in pursuance of an estimate which they had accepted, the proper inference was that there was a contract between the car owner and garage to repair the car at a price acceptable to the insurers within a reasonable time and also a contract between the garage and the insurers. Accordingly they went on, there was a contract between the car owner and the garage to repair the car within a reasonable time. This suggests that the court is likely to imply a term between Claimant and garage that repairs be completed within reasonable time.

Having established that there was a term requiring repairs to be effected in a reasonable time, the next question is how high the standard of care should be. Does the garage have to act in the same manner as a reasonable body of professional garages, by analogy with the medical negligence case law? Is the garage required to complete repairs within reasonable time or with reasonable expedition? The difference is that reasonable time simply refers to the passage of time whereas expedition puts the focus onto the garage's actions. There are no clear answers to these questions yet. In *Charnock* the court applied the standard of the "average competent repairer." It is clear however that there is not an implied term that the repairs will be completed in accordance with the time estimate: this would not be commercially realistic.

Whether or not repairs have been completed within reasonable time or with reasonable expedition is a question of fact which will depend on the circumstances of the case.

There may also be issues regarding whether hire charges would be a recoverable head of loss under the rule in *Hadley* v *Baxendale* 9 Exch 341, or otherwise under causation, remoteness or foreseeability.

Claiming a Contribution from the Claimant's Insurer

Defendants may wonder whether, if they can claim a contribution from a garage which causes delay, they can also claim a contribution against a Claimant's insurer who delays processing the claim.

To succeed, the Defendant would need to show that the Claimant could successfully claim damages against their own insurer. This would entail:

> i) showing that there was an express / implied term in the Claimant's insurance contract stating that the insurer will act with reasonable expedition;

ii) showing that there is an action for consequential losses as a result of breaching such a term;

iii) showing on the facts that the insurer breached the term and that the breach caused the Claimant loss.

In the absence of an express term stating that the insurer will handle claims efficiently and in default will be liable for consequential losses (and we are not aware of any insurance contracts with such an express term), the Defendant can only argue that there is an implied term in the insurance contract that the insurer will act with reasonable expedition.

A Defendant is likely to face considerable difficulties in establishing such an implied term. In Insurance Corporation of the *Channel Islands* v *McHugh (No 1)* [1997] LRLR 94, Mance J held that an insurer does not owe an implied duty to conduct negotiations, assessed the amount due or make payment within a reasonable time. He considered that such a term could not be implied either as a matter of business efficacy or as a matter of mutual intention.

Furthermore, the present position is that an insured cannot recover damages for consequential losses arising out of late payment of an insurance claim. The reason is that the insurer is liable to indemnify the insured from the moment of loss. It is therefore liable in damages from that moment. The only remedy for late payment of damages is interest, because it is not possible to recover further damages for losses arising out of the late payment of damages. Where an insurer delays paying a claim, the only remedy available to the insured is interest. Relevant caselaw includes *Sprung* v *Royal Insurance* [1999] Lloyds Rep IR 111 followed in *Tonkin* v *UK Insurance Ltd* [2006] EWHC 1120 TCC among others.

It is also not possible to claim damages for inconvenience or distress arising out of late payment of insurance claims. The reasons are that an insurance contract is not considered a contract to secure peace of mind and that the only remedy for late payment is interest. See for instance *Ventouris* v *Mountain* [1992] 2 Lloyds Rep 281.

Thus the law at present stands against the Defendant. It would take a House of Lords decision or Parliament to reform the law. However, there are signs that change might be forthcoming. The Court of Appeal in *Mandrake Holding Ltd* v *Countrywide Assurance Group Plc* [2005] EWCA Civ 840 indicated that the House of Lords might revisit the law in this area. Similarly concerns have been expressed in a 2006 Law Commission report and in academic articles about the state of the law in this area.

There may also be a specific clause in the insurance policy excluding liability for consequential loss. Depending on the precise wording of the exclusion clause, this might operate to limit liability for breach of any implied term.

If the Defendant succeeds in establishing that there was such an implied term in the Claimant's insurance policy, it would then have to establish that the insurer breached that term and that the breach caused the Claimant increased loss. This will inevitably be fact sensitive. It is unlikely that every administrative delay would be held to be a breach of contract: the courts would be sensitive to commercial realities. Clearly the Defendant's argument becomes more attractive the more severe the delay. Further there is a practical difficulty for Defendants in that all the evidence about the alleged delay would be held by the Claimant's insurer.

Claimant's car written off

Issues relating to the period of hire may also arise where the Claimant's vehicle is written off in the accident. Claimants often hire a vehicle until the Defendant insurer refunds them the pre-accident value of the vehicle to enable them to purchase a new vehicle. Sometimes the hire charges incurred dwarf the pre-accident value of the Claimant's vehicle. Here it is simply a question of reasonableness on the facts of each particular case. All the general principles of mitigation cited above apply here.

Defendants may point to the case of *Fettes* v *Williams* (22 January 2003) in which the Claimant's car was damaged in a road traffic accident. The cost of repairs was £1,880. She hired a replacement vehicle for 10 months at a total cost of £15,517. The Claimant argued that she could not afford the repairs. On the facts it was held that she could have found the money somehow. The decision is interesting because the court was willing to take into account her partner's income. The result was that hire was only recovered for a period of two months. HHJ Hull QC also commented that, if on the facts the Claimant had not been able to raise the money, "then I would go further and hold that the chain of causation of her loss must, after a reasonable period, perhaps a few months, be broken by Hamco's insouciant and cheerful agreement to go on providing indemnity for an indefinite period of hire".

The following quotation from Pearson LJ in *Derbyshire* v *Warren*, admittedly in a slightly different context, may be cited by Defendants:

> He was fully entitled to have his damaged vehicle repaired at whatever cost because he preferred it. But he was not justified in charging against the defendant the cost of repairing the damaged vehicle when that cost was more than twice the replacement market value and he had made no attempt to find a replacement vehicle.

Claimants may obviously argue that the threshold of mitigation is very low. It is arguable that it is only their own financial situation which should be taken into account and not their partner's. Furthermore that as a matter of fact causation continued.

5. Different cars

Another issue which arose in *Burdis* v *Livsey* was that one of the Claimants had his sports car damaged in an accident. He only hired a saloon as a replacement which was cheaper than a sports car would have been. The Court of Appeal held that:

> In the present case the loss suffered by Mr Dennard was the cost he had to pay for hire of the Vectra, not the amount which he might have paid for the hire of another car. A person who has no need for a replacement car because, for instance, he is abroad during the repair cannot recover the cost of hiring a replacement which he never incurs (see *Giles* v *Thompson* at 167D). Similarly, a person who does not incur the cost of hiring a sports car cannot recover more than the cost actually incurred.

6. Self-Employed Claimants

A separate issue of reasonableness can arise with self-employed Claimants who use their vehicle for their business. Suppose that the Claimant's business make a profit of £1,000 per month. Suppose further that the Claimant hires a replacement vehicle for work at a cost of £2,000 per month. If the Claimant were to pay the hire charges himself, that would mean that his business would be running at a loss of £1,000 per month. Defendants may argue that this is simply not reasonable. As the disparity in the figures grows, the Defendants argument becomes stronger.

Claimants may respond that the Defendant is effectively saying that it was unreasonable for them to carry on working following the accident. This comes back to the question how far a Claimant is expected to go to mitigate his loss. Is the Claimant required to give up his work for the Defendant's benefit?

It remains to be seen how the higher courts deal with this issue. The answer may simply be that it is a question of fact for the trial Judge to determine, having regard to the general principles of mitigation.

Chapter 11

MISCELLANEOUS

The preceding pages have traversed swathes of the credit hire countryside. The journey through this book is almost at an end. It only remains to cover a series of smaller self-contained topics, which crop up regularly in the authors' experience of credit hire practice.

Engineers' fees

Claimants frequently seek to recover the cost of instructing an engineer to inspect their damaged vehicle. Some cases suggest that engineers' fees may be recoverable if the report was necessary at the hearing but not if damages for the vehicle were not in dispute (see *Mistry* v *NE Computing* [1997] 5 CL 62, *Smith* v *Bogan & Sons Ltd* [1997] 11 CL 61, *Coleman* v *Stubbs* [1998] CLY 422, *Broderick* v *Jones* [1998] CLY 421, and *Pennant* v *Sparks* [1999] 1 CL).

In *Burdis* v *Livsey*, at paragraph 156 the Court of Appeal held:

> He [the Claimant] can recover the cost of the repair unless it be shown that he has not taken reasonable steps to mitigate his loss. Of course a number of quotations or one engineer's report can be good evidence to rebut an allegation of a failure to mitigate and may be useful in settlement negotiations; but the costs are not part of the loss. The fact that insurers use engineers to report on damaged cars and agree the costs of repair is irrelevant to the assessment of the amount of loss. Helphire use an engineer to negotiate the repair charges with the repairer with no doubt the view that the engineer's report will lead to a quick and satisfactory settlement of the claim and protect Helphire. As such they would not be recoverable.

This built on earlier discussion in *Seddon* v *Tekin* and *Dowsett* v *Clifford*, HHJ Harris, Oxford County Court, 25 August 2001, HHJ Harris took a different approach and stated (at page 64):

> Is it a recoverable head of damage at all or is it one of the additional benefits referred to by Lord Hoffman, I think it is the latter, It is saving the Claimant the trouble of taking his car round several garages in order to get competitive quotations and so decide whether the price at which the car is mended is reasonable. Accordingly on the authority of *Dimond* I hold that the cost of a repair assessor is non recoverable.

Note further that where proceedings are brought simply to recover an engineer's fee, this has been held to be an abuse of the process of the court in issuing solely to recover costs (see *Warriner* v *Smith* [1999] 4 CL (effectively, the test case on this issue: see note of Dominic Adamson, Barrister), *Malone* v *Button* [1998] CLY 495, *Video Box Office Limited* v *GST Holdings* [1990] The Independent, CA, *Scarrott* v *Staiton* [1989], unreported, CA and *Hobbs* v *Marlowe* [1978] AC 16).

Inconvenience and miscellaneous expenses

Claims for the inconvenience associated with the accident and for miscellaneous expenses such as postage and telephone costs for pursuing the claim are often tagged on to a credit hire claim. In this regard, Scott V–C in *Dimond* approved the assertion "that damages for worry and for the nuisance caused by having to deal with the consequences of an accident are not recoverable." This follows from *Nicholls* v *Rushton* [1992] CLY 3252 in which it was held that there could be no claim for inconvenience without some form of medical injury. This is also supported by *Taylor* v *Browne* [1995] CLY 1842.

As regards claims for miscellaneous expenses, *Taylor* v *Browne* suggests that these would not be recoverable since they are effectively a claim for costs. *Marley* v *Novak* [1996] CLY 2112 suggests that miscellaneous expenses may be claimed. *O'Brien* v *King-Phillips* [1997] 1814 takes a middle line and suggests that such a claim may be sustainable if it is related to the actual damage, for example money lost in visiting a repairing garage.

Storage and Recovery Charges

Very often a claim is made for storage and recovery charges. There is nothing wrong with such a claim in principle but if there has been a deferment of the debt in any way or any assurances as to the absence of personal liability for example, the basis of the agreement may be open to similar criticisms as those applied to credit hire and repair.

Again, the primary issue is to determine for what the Claimant contracted, when and with whom and then to ask whether he is liable for anything on that contract. Unlike credit hire contracts, there is often no written agreement between Claimant and company for storage charges. This means that if there is a deferment of the debt, the contract may well be unenforceable under the Consumer Credit Act.

Furthermore issues of mitigation may arise. The Defendant may argue that it was open to the Claimant to store the vehicle at his house. The value of the car is also relevant. It may well be argued that it is unreasonable, for example, to incur storage charges which approach or exceed the value of the vehicle.

Potentially Claimants may be able to argue that the vehicle is being stored pending the Defendant insurer inspecting the vehicle. If this is correct then the responsibility for any delay rests with the Defendant.

Delivery and Collection Charges

Similar arguments may arise with regard to delivery and collection charges for the credit hire vehicle. Issues may also arise as to whether these constitute "additional benefits" which may not be recovered post-*Dimond*.

In *Miller* v *Hulbert*, DJ Jackson; Romford County Court; 15 May 2000, the District Judge held that following *Dimond*, the Claimant was not entitled to recover the cost of collection/delivery or CDW as they were "additional benefits".

In *Clark* v *Ardington Electrical Services and others*, HHJ Harris, Oxford County Court, 14 September 2001, HHJ Harris stated:

> ...Delivery is manifestly a convenience. Many companies do not offer delivery, others do, at widely differing rates. According to Mr Mainz 62% would deliver, the majority of those that did would do so for free. But in the light of the Dimond decision I do not think that delivery charges can be generally recoverable in ordinary cases, since convenient delivery is an additional benefit to the use of the car, and going to get a hire car is presumably part of what the Vice Chancellor called the "nuisance caused by having to deal with the consequences of an accident". [2001] 1 QB 216, 219.

However, he went on to say:

> However, for some people it may reasonably be necessary to have a delivery if for example the victim was handicapped or had no practicable or cheaper way of getting to the car himself. A long taxi ride might cost more than a delivery charge, in which case the latter should be recoverable.

The issue of delivery and collection charges was dealt with in *Burdis* v *Livsey*. Before the Court of Appeal all the parties agreed that these charges would sometimes be recoverable. At paragraph 153 the Court defined those circumstances in which delivery and collection would be recoverable:

If injury causes damage then the injured party can recover the loss caused by the injury. But the need for a replacement car is not self-proving (see Giles v Thompson at 167 D); neither is the need for delivery self-proving. If the injured person lives next door to the car hire company, he can walk round and collect the replacement car and a delivery and collection charge is not part of the loss. However, the cost of obtaining the replacement car can be recovered subject to the duty to take reasonable steps to mitigate the loss. What is reasonable is a question of fact, which can usually be deduced from the surrounding circumstances. If there is suitable public transport, it would be reasonable to expect the car to be collected. If part of the loss is the cost of delivery and collection, that must be proved.

Collision Damage Waiver

Are Collision Damage Waiver charges levied by hire companies recoverable from the Defendant? In *Marcic v Davies*, Court of Appeal 20 February 1985, the Defendant sought to argue that collision damage waiver incorporated an element of betterment. Browne-Wilkinson LJ held that:

> I do not accept that submission. In accordance with the ordinary rule of damages the plaintiff is entitled to be put back, as far as possible, into the position in which he would have been had the collision not occurred. If there had been no collision the plaintiff would never have come under any contractual liability to the car hire company. It was accepted that it was reasonable for him to hire the car from the car hire company. Since he could only do this by effecting comprehensive insurance in the full amount or by bearing the excess of £150, if he had elected to bear the excess himself, he would, under the terms of his hiring contract with the hire company, have come under a contractual liability to pay £150 to the hire company in respect of damage. What is more, that would be damage not to his own motor car but to hire company's motor car. Accordingly, this liability for £150 that he would have had to the hire company if he had not paid the waiver fee would have been a contractual obligation which he would never have been under had it not been for the original collision with the defendant...

> The element of betterment to which Mr Tudor Evans referred would only have arisen if during the period of the hire the plaintiff had in fact had a further accident. It is true that if that had happened to his own motor car he would have had to bear the wh0ole cost of the damage to his motor car if he had decided to have it repaired, whereas if the hired car had crashed during that period he would not have had to bear such cost. But in fact no such accident occurred. What we are concerned wit is the cost of covering the plaintiff against a contractual liability that he was bound to enter into and the cost of so doing. In my judgment the learned judge was right to include the waiver fee as an item of recoverable damage.

The point was revisited in *Bee* v *Jenson* [2006] EWHC 3359 before Morison J. He commented that "had the point been live, I would have held that it was reasonable for the replacement vehicle to have been provided with a nil excess regardless of the excess that applied to Mr Bee's own car." His reasoning was that rather than being a betterment, the collision damage waiver is a reasonable arrangement consequential on the tort.

He also referred to *Marcic* v *Davies*. He accepted that the case was binding on him and added "I have no hesitation in following it".

Credit Repair

In previous editions of this book, this merited a whole chapter of its own. However the status of credit repair agreements should no longer be controversial following *Burdis* v *Livsey*. The question had always been whether it was possible to treat credit repair agreements differently from credit hire agreements, because repairs represent a direct loss. In *Burdis* the CA answered this question beginning at paragraph 84:

> In our judgment a fundamental distinction must be drawn, for present purposes, between repair costs and hire charges. When a vehicle is damaged by the negligence of a third party, the owner suffers an immediate loss representing the diminution in value of the vehicle. As a general rule, the measure of that damage is the cost of carrying out the repairs necessary to restore the vehicle to its pre-accident condition (see *Dimond* at page 1139G per Lord Hobhouse).

> 85. In *Burdis* the general rule applied, and it was common ground that the repairs restored Miss Burdis' car to its pre-accident value. Nor was there any issue as to the reasonableness of the garage's charges. Thus at the moment when the accident occurred Miss Burdis suffered a direct and immediate loss, the measure of which was the cost of the repairs which were in fact carried out (£2,981.19). But it was not a condition precedent to the recovery of compensation for that loss that the car be repaired: Miss Burdis' cause of action for the recovery of damages representing the diminution in the value of her car caused by Mr Livsey's negligence was complete when the accident occurred (see: *The Glenfinlas* [1918] P363 and The London Corporation [1935] P 70 CA). Similarly, a claimant's damages will not be affected by the fact that, in the event, the repairs are carried out at no cost to him (see *The Endeavour* (1890) 6 Asp MC 511, where the vessel was repaired but, due to the bankruptcy of the owner, the repairer was never paid).

> 86. By contrast, the hire charges which were sought to be recovered in *Dimond* represented a potential future loss, consequent upon the defendant's tort, which was recoverable as damages only if and when it was

in fact suffered. In the language of pleading, the hire charges constituted special damage. As Judge Harris put it in *Seddon* (at page 2890), in the passage quoted earlier, the hire charges are "of the essence of the damage which is consequential loss or special damage". Hence in *Dimond*, because the credit hire agreement was unenforceable and the hire charges were accordingly irrecoverable from the claimant, the hire charges never formed part of the claimant's loss.

The Court of Appeal continued:

> 91. In our judgment, the authorities to which we have so far referred establish that subsequent events which are not referable in a causative sense to the commission of the tort, that is to say events which, on a true analysis, are collateral to the commission of the tort, or *res inter alios acta*, or too remote - we regard these expressions as interchangeable - do not affect the measure of a direct loss suffered when the tort was committed.
>
> 92. In the case of potential future losses, on the other hand, the general rule is that to the extent that such a loss is in fact avoided (for whatever reason) it is a loss which is never suffered and which is accordingly irrecoverable for that reason.

Accordingly the Court of Appeal decided that:

> 104. In our judgment the agreement between Miss Burdis and Accident Assistance was plainly collateral to the tort, and must accordingly be left out of account in assessing Miss Burdis' damages. We do not see how it could be said that the agreement flowed from any act of mitigation by Miss Burdis - rather, it flowed from the fact that Mr Livsey's insurers had not settled the claim. The true analysis, in our judgment, is that Miss Burdis has discharged her contractual obligation to the garage to pay for the repairs. The fact that she has done so by arranging for the payment to be made by a third party (Accident Assistance) seems to us to be irrelevant in the context of assessment of damages.

The result is a clearcut distinction between credit repair and credit hire. Credit repair charges are in principle recoverable, regardless of the Consumer Credit Act issues.

Interest

Can Claimants recover interest on credit hire charges? In *Giles* v *Thompson* [1994] AC 142, Lord Mustill said (at page 168), of the award of interest, "The exercise of the right should correspond with reality". In that case there was no liability to pay the hire charges until judgment was given and therefore no award of interest was made.

However, if insurers have already re-imbursed the credit hire company, they may then potentially be entitled to interest.

In *Clark* v *Ardington Electrical Services and others*, HHJ Harris, Oxford County Court, 14 September 2001, HHJ Harris allowed interest to be awarded to a subrogated Claimant from the date of payment. He referred to *Cousins* v *D & C* [1971] 1All ER 55 CA and stated:

> There is of course no doubt that as far as the Defendants are concerned, if the claimants had paid for the car repairs and hire themselves they would have been entitled to interest. I see no reason in principle or in commonsense why the Defendants should be relieved of that liability because the claimants have arranged the repairs and hire via Helphire. Accordingly, I find the position analogous to that in Cousins, and would award interest, in the cases where the claimants succeed, from the dates upon which the payments in respect of repair and hire were made.

HHJ Harris' decision was upheld on this point in *Burdis* v *Livsey* at paragraphs 157 - 162. The result is this: if the hire charges have been paid (e.g. by the insurer in the Helphire scheme), interest is recoverable.

Some credit hire contracts now include provision for contractual interest. It is open to Defendants to argue that this is not recoverable because it represents an additional charge for hiring on credit pursuant to *Dimond* v *Lovell.*

Claimants may point to Lord Mustill's speech in *Giles* v *Thompson*, where in giving judgment on interest he distinguished the position in that case from that where contractual interest is due. Also potentially impecuniosity may assist the Claimant.

Chapter 12

OTHER REGULATORY REGIMES

We are grateful to Roland Waters and Anthony Johnson for providing the ideas and the research which inspired this chapter.

This Chapter deals with two other regulatory regimes that might potentially be relevant to credit hire litigation: the Financial Services regime and the Data Protection regime.

The Financial Services Authority

Background

The Financial Services Authority (FSA) is an independent body that regulates the financial services industry in the United Kingdom. It exercises statutory powers given to it by the Financial Services and Markets Act 2000 and acts as a single regulator for the financial services industry. This chapter looks at one particular aspect of its regulation, that over insurance companies and so-called 'third party capture'. Questions such as who else might be caught by the regulations might also arise but are beyond the scope of this introductory chapter though may well end up being relevant in themselves.

Financial Services and Markets Act 2000

Section 2(1) of the 2000 Act provides that:

> "In discharging its general functions [the FSA] must, so far as is reasonably possible, act in a way-
>
> > a) which is compatible with the regulatory objectives; and
> >
> > b) which [the FSA] considers most appropriate for the purpose of meeting those objectives.

Section 2(2) outlines the four regulatory objectives of the FSA which are:

- market confidence;
- public awareness;
- the protection of consumers; and
- the reduction of financial crime.

"The protection of consumers" is the most relevant in the context of credit hire litigation. The FSA also considers this to be its most important function (*c.f.* for example "The Future Regulation of Insurance" 20 November 2001).

These statutory objectives are supported by a set of Principles of good regulation, which the FSA must take into account when discharging its functions. These are contained in section 2(3) of the Act and are as follows:

> a) the need to use its resources in the most efficient and economic way;
> b) the responsibilities of those who manage the affairs of authorised persons;
> c) the principle that a burden or restriction which is imposed on a person or on the carrying on of an activity, should be proportionate to the benefits, considered in general terms, which are expected to result from the imposition of that burden or restriction;
> d) the desirability of facilitating innovation in connection with regulated activities;
> e) the international character of financial services and markets and the desirability of maintaining the competitive position of the United Kingdom;
> f) the need to minimise the adverse effects on competition that may arise from anything done in the discharge of those functions
> g) the desirability of facilitating competition between those who are subject to any form of regulation by [the FSA].

The FSA places a great deal of importance on these Principles: its Managing Director for Retail Markets has argued that such a principles-based (as opposed to 'rules-based') approach actually strengthens its consumer protection goals, saying, "Our principles are rules. We can take enforcement action on the basis of them; we have already done so; and we intend increasingly to do so where it is appropriate to do so".

The 2000 statute only provides a skeletal regulatory framework within which the FSA operates. The detail is contained in the FSA's *Handbook of Rules and Guidance* which sets out in full the standards which the financial industry must comply with and guidance upon those standards. The Handbook is most conveniently available online and is updated daily.

There is a great deal of material available both online and in other formats about the FSA regulatory regime. We set out below some of the sections which may be relevant in a credit hire context.

Principles for Businesses

The FSA Handbook sets out principles that are "a general statement of the fundamental obligations of firms under the regulatory system. They derive their authority from the FSA's rule-making powers as set out in the [2000

Act] and reflect the regulatory objectives." The Principles are stated to "apply in whole or in part to every firm" with respect to the carrying on of "regulated activities." The Handbook's Glossary confirms that regulated activities include "effecting contracts of insurance" and "carrying out contracts of insurance".

The Principles themselves are outlined in full in the FSA Handbook at PRIN 2.1:

> 1. Integrity: A firm must conduct its business with integrity
> 2. Skill, care and diligence: A firm must conduct its business with due skill, care and diligence
> 3. Management and control: A firm must take reasonable care to organise and control its affairs responsibly and effectively, with adequate risk management systems
> 4. Financial prudence: A firm must maintain adequate financial resources
> 5. Market conduct: A firm must observe proper standards of market conduct
> 6. Customers' interests: A firm must pay due regard to the interests of its customers and treat them fairly
> 7. Communication with clients: A firm must pay due regard to the information needs of its clients, and communicate information to them in a way which is clear, fair and not misleading
> 8. Conflicts of interest: A firm must manage conflicts of interest fairly, both between itself and its customers and between a customer and another client
> 9. Customers: relationships of trust: A firm must take reasonable care to ensure the suitability of its advice and discretionary decisions for any customer who is entitled to rely upon its judgment
> 10. Clients' assets: A firm must arrange adequate protection for clients' assets when it is responsible for them
> 11. Relations with regulators: A firm must deal with its regulators in an open and cooperative way, and must disclose to the FSA appropriately anything relating to the firm of which the FSA would reasonably expect.

Insurance: Conduct of Business (ICOB)

Chapter 1 of ICOB explains that its purpose is to implement the provisions of a number of EC Directives. The section most relevant to the credit hire industry is Chapter 7 entitled 'Claims Handling'. This outlines the following requirements:-

> 7.3.1 An insurer must carry out claims handling promptly and fairly.
>
> ...

7.3.5 When an insurer is informed that a customer wishes to claim under his policy it must give the customer reasonable guidance to help him make a claim under his policy.

...

7.3.6(1) An insurer must not unreasonably reject a claim made by a customer.

To whom does the FSA Handbook apply?

ICOB 7.1.1 makes it clear that the handbook applies to insurers. It also applies to "an insurance intermediary" and "a managing agent". Their definition may be the scope of some debate in itself and is not covered by this introductory chapter though it may well in itself end up being relevant.

What does the FSA Handbook cover?

The provisions of the FSA Handbook are not of general application. An entity covered by the above regulations only owes obligations to certain individuals and not to the general population.

Claims by Policyholders

ICOB 1.2.5 states that "All Chapters of ICOB are relevant to a firm that deals with a retail customer". ICOB 1.2.5A goes on to say:

> (1) In ICOB 2 (General rules) and ICOB 7 (Claims handling (and in ICOB 1 (Application and purpose) in respect of those chapters), a customer is a policyholder or a prospective policyholder. Otherwise, only a policyholder or prospective policyholder who makes the arrangements preparatory to him concluding the contract of insurance (directly or through an agent) is a customer.

> (2) A policyholder includes anyone who, upon the occurrence of the contingency insured against, is entitled to make a claim directly to the insurance undertaking.

It is clear from these provisions that the full force of the regulatory regime, applies to insurers in respect of their dealings with their own policyholders. The definition of 'policyholder' is relatively wide: it is capable of including named drivers on an insurance policy for example.

Third Party Capture

A so-called 'third party capture' arrangement arises when an insurance company (or their agent) deals directly with a customer of another insurance company (or other third party) who brings / may bring a claim against it in the future.

ICOB 7.2.2 states:

> When an insurer deals directly with a third party who claims against his customer because the third party has a legal right to bypass the customer and claim directly against the insurer (for example, certain motor claims or because of the insolvency of the customer), these rules do not require the insurer to treat the third party as a customer. However, the insurer should have regard to Principle 1 (Integrity), Principle 2 (Skill, care and diligence) and Principle 5 (Market conduct) in its dealing with the third party and should not deal with the claim in any way less favourably than it would have done had the claim been proceeded against its customer.

This ensures that insurance companies, or any other entity regulated by the FSA, should comply with the stated three Principles in their dealings with third parties. That insurers were covered for third-party capture was dealt with in a debate in the House of Lords in considering a draft exemption order under the Compensation Act 2006. Baroness Ashton of Upholland, Parliamentary Under Secretary of State to the DCA, stated in an open letter to Lord Goodhart that:

> The FSA has clarified that the handling of insurance claims by insurers is regulated under the Financial Services and Markets Act 2000, including where the insurer deals directly with a third party who has a claim against its policyholder. The regulation of these activities therefore falls within the FSA's remit and does not need to be subject to additional regulation within the scope of the Compensation Act 2006.

> The FSA has stated that it will consider any evidence submitted to it that suggests impropriety on the part of its authorised firms to determine whether action needs to be taken in respect of any individual firms. We intend to inform respondents to the consultation who specifically raised issues concerning the service provided by insurers that they should raise concerns with the FSA. The FSA would of course also consider via its normal procedures whether there is a case for the application of additional rules.

The Consequences of Breaches of the FSA Handbook

Breaches in the Context of Existing Litigation

This may well end up being the subject of some debate. Imagine for the sake of argument that a Defendant insurer in a credit hire case was in breach of its obligations to a third party, *i.e.* the Claimant. How would this impact on the litigation? The Claimant might potentially argue that the Defendant should not be allowed to run any argument that depended in whole or in part on its own breach of obligations under the FSA regime. In effect this would be running some form of public policy, illegality or estoppel-type argument. Alternatively, Claimants may prefer the slightly different tack of simply pointing out that it ill behoves a Defendant who has breached its obligations, to argue that the Claimant has committed a relatively trivial failure to mitigate. Seen in this light, the Claimant would essentially be inviting the court (particularly when considering mitigation) to consider all the facts and circumstances of a case before reaching a conclusion. Breaches of the regulatory regime might potentially be a relevant part of the factual matrix. Such breaches may be pleaded, for example in a Reply.

For Defendants responding to such an argument, it may be argued that breaches of the regulatory regime are just not relevant to the issues in the litigation itself. If the Defendant has unduly delayed for example, the court can consider this anyway without reference to the regulatory regime.

Ultimately, these issues might also become relevant in relation to costs.

Outside Litigation

Beyond any litigation itself, there remain the various avenues of complaint for individuals who feel that an obligation to them has been breached. For example, it is possible that a breach of the FSA Handbook could give rise to grounds for a complaint to the FSA. The Handbook empowers the FSA to impose disciplinary measures to further the FSMA 2000 scheme. The Introduction to the Enforcement section of the FSA explains the rationale behind the imposition of such measures:

> Disciplinary measures are one of the regulatory tools available to the FSA. They are not the only tool, and it may be appropriate to address many instances of non-compliance without recourse to disciplinary action. However, the effective and proportionate use of the FSA's powers to enforce the requirements of the Act, the rules and the Statements of Principle will play an important role in buttressing the FSA's pursuit of its regulatory objectives. The imposition of disciplinary measures (that is, financial penalties, public censures and public statements) shows that regulatory standards are being upheld and helps to maintain market confidence, promote public awareness of regulatory standards and deter financial crime.

An increased public awareness of regulatory standards also contributes to the protection of consumers.

The Handbook is clear that there are situations when it is permissible to discipline a firm for the breach of a Principle alone, even in the absence of the breach of a Rule. It is stated that "the Principles are a general statement of the fundamental obligations of firms under the regulatory system"; this accords with the FSA's stated aim for 'principles-based' regulation.

The FSA Handbook provides guidance on determining whether or not a Principle has been breached:

> In determining whether a Principle has been broken, it is necessary to look to the standard of conduct required by the Principle in question. Under each of the Principles, the onus will be on the FSA to show that a firm has been at fault in some way. This requirement will differ depending upon the Principle: for example, under Principle 1, the FSA must show that a firm has failed to conduct its business with integrity; under Principle 2, the FSA must prove that the firm http://fsahandbook.info/FSA/glossary-html/handbook/Glossary/F?definition=G430 has failed to act with due skill, care and diligence in the conduct of its business.

The next paragraph provides guidance on situations in which disciplinary action can be brought for breach of a Principle alone:

> In certain cases it may be appropriate to discipline a firm on the basis of the Principle alone. Examples include the following:
> (1) where there is no detailed rule which prohibits the behaviour in question, but the behaviour clearly contravenes a Principle.
> (2) where a firm has committed a number of breaches of detailed rules which individually may not merit disciplinary action, but the cumulative effect of which indicates the breach of a Principle.

For further details of the FSA's enforcement powers, see the Enforcement Section of the FSA Handbook.

In light of the above it might be that the threshold to persuade the FSA to impose a public censure or a financial penalty is not met in an individual case and it may well be that the FSA will instead issue a private warning than either of the more severe, publicised, sanctions. However, the FSA might be persuaded to impose more serious sanctions in respect of a repeat offender who had had a warning, or warnings, before, or if a complaint were made alleging breaches of the Principles and/or Rules in numerous different cases involving the same two firms, e.g. a large insurer and a large credit hire firm. However, all cases will depend upon their individual facts.

It is also worth noting at this stage that although the FSA can penalise the wrongdoer, there is no provision allowing compensation to the victim.

A Complaint to the Ombudsman

It is possible that a party could make a complaint to the Financial Ombudsman Service. The Ombudsman was established by the FSMA 2000 to replace six former schemes operating in various sectors of the financial industry. Since 1st December 2001 complaints under its jurisdiction have been dealt with by the Ombudsman in accordance with the 'Dispute Resolution: Complaints' (DISP) section of the FSA Handbook.

The Ombudsman procedure is relatively informal, and is designed chiefly to be used in situations where a customer makes a complaint against a firm. It is usually a condition precedent of the Ombudsman becoming involved that the customer has first attempted to deal with the company through its own complaints procedure. The Ombudsman does not have a role to play in disputes between large companies; it only has jurisdiction to look at complaints from small businesses with a turnover of less than £1,000,000 and the maximum award that it can make is £100,000

The Ombudsman is a potentially useful tool for individuals who have been wronged by an FSA-regulated firm. It is unlikely that any damages awarded by the Ombudsman would be much more than nominal, as there are few situations when it is envisaged that a tangible loss could be attributed to the firms' breach of the rules or guidance. Nevertheless, the costs involved in dealing with a claim to the Ombudsman, both financial and in terms of time and inconvenience, should not be underestimated; it is certainly something that firms would wish to avoid if it all possible.

Conclusion

It remains to be seen whether the FSA rules start to become relevant to litigation both in credit hire and beyond in, for example personal injury and other insurance-based litigation. It is hoped that this article has at least given a general introduction to some of the myriad issues which might arise.

Data Protection

Along with the FSA rules, the data protection jurisdiction is another which may potentially be relevant in certain cases. The Data Protection Act 1984 introduced formally into UK law eight Data Protection Principles, which derived from the European Convention on Protection of Personal Data 1981. Following further EU legislation, the law was reconciled in the Data Protection Act 1998 (DPA 1998).

Whilst the DPA 1998 remains the primary UK Data Protection legislation, the Human Rights Act 1998 has a direct impact on the storing, retention and access to personal information, as has the Freedom of Information Act 2000. The DPA 1998 must be interpreted in light of this further legislation.

The Data Protection Principles
The Data Protection Principles are set out in Part I of Schedule 1 to the DPA 1998; the Principles are to be interpreted in accordance with Part II of Schedule 1. Section 1 of the Act defines various terms that are used throughout the text of the Act.

1. Personal data shall be processed fairly and lawfully
Once it has been established that a person is entitled to process personal data, it is still necessary to ensure that the data is processed "fairly" and "lawfully". "Processing" is defined in section 1 of the DPA 1998. Further obligations apply in the case of "sensitive personal data" (as defined by section 2 of the Act)

2. Personal data shall be obtained for specified and lawful purposes and shall not be further processed in any manner incompatible with that purpose / purposes
Not only must the processing itself be lawful, and fair, but to comply with the Second Data Protection Principle, the data in question must be obtained solely for one or more specified lawful purpose or purposes.

3. Personal data shall be adequate, relevant and not excessive in relation to the purpose / purposes for which it is processed
In complying with this Principle, the OIC expects data controllers to identify the minimum amount of data that is required in order to properly fulfil their purpose. Accordingly, assessment of whether this Principle has been adhered to will be assessed on a case-by-case basis.

4. Personal data shall be accurate and, where necessary, kept up to date
Data will be deemed to be inaccurate if it is incorrect or misleading as to any matter of fact. The key requirement here is for data controllers to take reasonable steps to ensure the accuracy of the data obtained, held and processed, and to have in place control mechanisms to update the data where necessary. If a data subject identifies that inaccurate data is being held in relation to them, then pursuant to section 14 of the DPA 1998, the data subject can request that this be rectified, and the inaccurate data erased or destroyed.

5. Personal data shall not be kept for longer than is necessary for that purpose / purposes
The Fifth Data Protection Principle must be read in conjunction with the Second Data Protection Principle. The Fifth Principle requires that personal date is kept for no longer than is necessary for the specified and lawful purposes required by the Second Principle. The "necessary" amount of time is not defined in the Act although it may be self evidence from the nature of the lawful purpose.

6. Personal data shall be processed in accordance with the rights of the data subject under the Act
This Principle will only be breached if an organisation does not supply information in accordance with a subject access request or fails to comply with a Notice served under the Act. Examples of when such Notices might be served are to prevent processing likely to cause damage or distress, prevent processing for the purpose of direct marketing or to require the rectification or erasure of inaccurate or incomplete data.

7. Appropriate technical and organisational measures shall be taken against unauthorised or unlawful processing of personal data and against accidental loss, destruction or damage to personal data;
This essentially provides that all data controllers must put in place appropriate internal controls and security measures to prevent the above actions. There is no set security standard: it simply depends on all the circumstances of an individual case.

8. Personal data shall not be transferred to a country or territory outside the EEA without an adequate level of protection for the rights and freedoms of the data subject in relation to the processing of personal data
It is unlikely that this Principle will need to be considered in most cases where all the data generated is handled within the UK. However, in situations where data is put beyond the EEA then this may well be a highly relevant topic. Schedule 4 of the DPA 1998 outlines cases where the Eighth Principle does not apply.

Other Provisions of the DPA 1998
In addition to enshrining the Data Protection Principles into English law, the data protection regime under the DPA 1998, contains several other relevant provisions.

Notification
A data controller has to "notify" the OIC that it intends to perform that function under the Act. Notification is dealt with in detail under Part III of the DPA 1998, sections 16 – 26.

It is an offence not only to process data without registration but also to fail to notify changes in the organisations status or the purposes for which data is to be processed within the organisation to the Registrar. Breach of this obligation is treated seriously by the OIC. In March 2005 a firm of solicitors was fined £3,150 for failing to notify / register with the Information Commissioner stating that:

> Complying with the Data Protection Act ensures that individuals' personal information is secure, accurate, up-to-date and is processed fairly. This prosecution should remind solicitors and other organisations of their responsibilities under the Act.

Subject Access
'Subject Access', dealt with at Sections 6 – 9 of the Act, entitles an individual, upon making a request in writing and paying the appropriate fee, to be told by the data controller whether they or someone else on their behalf is processing that individual's personal data, and if so to be given a description of the data itself, the purpose for which it is being processed and those to whom the data has been or may be disclosed.

The individual data subject is also entitled to have communicated to him all the information which forms any such personal data. This must be provided in permanent form by way of a copy save where the data cannot be provided in a permanent form, or where to do so would involve disproportionate effort. "Disproportionate effort" is not defined in the Act and is, therefore, a matter for assessment on a case-by-case basis. This will be a question of balancing the needs of the data subject against the time, cost and difficulty of compiling the copy information.

A data controller is not required to comply with a request where they have already complied with a similar or identical request from the same data subject unless a reasonable period has elapsed between such requests. The question of what will be deemed a reasonable period will again be a matter for assessment on a case by case basis.

Exemptions
Part IV, sections 28-36 of the Act, together with Schedule 7, outline the exemptions to the Act. They are numerous. Relevant exemptions include:

- Data required by law or in connection with legal proceedings (section 35);
- Records of the intentions of the data controller in relation to any negotiations with the data subject (Schedule 7, para. 7);
- Data that is subject to Legal Professional Privilege (Schedule 7, para. 10);
- Information available under an enactment (section 34); and
- Information processed for the purpose of the prevention or detection of crime, and / or the apprehension or prosecution of offenders (section 29).

Sanctions and Penalties
If a data subject believes that a data controller is processing data in a way that is likely to cause them substantial unwarranted damage or damage and distress, section 10 of the DPA 1998 provides that the subject may serve notice on the controller requiring them, within a reasonable time, to stop the processing activities. This is known as a "Data Subject Notice".

If such a notice is served, then the data controller must, within 21 days, give the data subject written notice stating either that he has complied with the Notice or intends to comply with it, or outlining the extent to which he intends to comply with it, if at all, and if not the parts of the Notice he considers unjustified.

If this results in a dispute between the data controller and the data subject, there are three usual outcomes. Firstly, that the subject issues civil proceedings against the controller, either simply for compensation or also for a declaration that there has been a breach of the Act. In order for such a complainant to be awarded compensation he must establish that he has suffered damage or damage and distress, which is both substantial and unwarranted. These are not specifically defined and will require assessment on a case-by-case basis. Secondly, the data subject may make a complaint to the OIC alleging breach of the Act and requesting that the OIC investigate the same. The OIC has substantial enforcement powers which are set out at Part V of the Act. Finally, the parties may agree a settlement by negotiation.

The Role of Data Protection in Credit Hire Litigation
Currently Data Protection arguments rarely arise in credit hire litigation. We set out below instances where Data Protection issues could be relevant. These are not intended to be either definitive or exhaustive but merely reflections as to potential issues which may potentially arise.

First it is important that any organisation that stores personal data registers as a data controller in accordance with the requirements of Part III of the

DPA 1998; anecdotal evidence suggests that in practice this is frequently overlooked.

Second, it is possible that breaches of the Data Protection Principles may be committed in the course of litigation. Particularly relevant are the principles that data be processed fairly and that personal data processed is relevant and not excessive. It may be that breaches of these principles are often overlooked. However if the data subject feels that their personal data is being used improperly, they can issue separate civil proceedings or complain to the OIC. This could be an effective way to police the use of personal data in civil proceedings.

Third, the subject access provisions (set out above) could be used for one party to the litigation to find out exactly what information is held on them by the other party. Of course it is possible under the Civil Procedure Rules to ask for disclosure under Part 31. However the disclosure provisions are relatively restrictive: they only apply for example to material relevant to the litigation. Under the Data Protection Act a much wider range of information would have to be provided.

It is less clear whether breaches of the Data Protection Act could ever be directly relevant to credit hire litigation. It might be possible (by analogy to the arguments under the FSA above) to argue that it ill behoves a Defendant who has breached the Data Protection principles to argue for example that the Claimant has failed to respond quickly enough to requests for information. Even if such an argument would not get off the ground, breaches of the Data Protection Act may still potentially sound in costs subject to the particular facts of each case.

Conclusion

In both *Lagden* v *O'Connor* and *Burdis* v *Livsey*, the very highest courts in the land confidently predicted that their decisions would not lead to increased litigation in small cases. They were wrong. Quantum only credit hire cases continue to abound in County Courts up and down the country. Many such cases are on the fast track or small claims track.

It is correct that following *Dimond* v *Lovell* most of the old Consumer Credit Act arguments are no longer relevant. All the larger credit hire organisations have carefully crafted terms and conditions that are exempt from regulation under the consumer credit legislation. Occasionally, however new arguments do still arise on the construction of the legislation and it remains important to have an awareness of the whole legislative background.

In the main the battleground has moved on to issues of mitigation of loss and additional benefits / impecuniosity. This does not mean the battle is any less fierce. There is still scope for specialists in this field to maintain a competitive advantage. In many respects, this book simply highlights the range of conflicting decisions at County Court level on these issues.

There are also new arguments waiting to be explored. It remains to be seen what impact the Unfair Terms in Consumer Contracts Regulations 1999, the Financial Services Authority and even the Consumer Credit Act 2006 have on credit hire litigation. The incentive to broach new arguments is clear: a decisive point could be worth millions of pounds to insurers or to hire companies.

Index

Lightning Source UK Ltd.
Milton Keynes UK
UKOW031318121211

183644UK00005B/8/P